God

in the picture

snapshots from a four-time
cancer survivor's life

t. windahl

Beaver's Pond Press, Inc.
Edina, Minnesota

ISBN 1-59298-038-4

Library of Congress Catalog Number: 2003115641

Printed in the United States of America

First Printing: January 2004

08 07 06 05 04   5 4 3 2 1

Beaver's Pond Press, Inc.   7104 Ohms Lane, Suite 216, Edina, MN 55439
(952) 829-8818
www.beaverspondpress.com

to order, visit *www.BookHouseFulfillment.com* or call
1-800-901-3480. Reseller discounts available.

Dedication

To Pete, the one who has shown me the true meaning of love and commitment.

To Zach, the one who constantly amazes me with his generous and compassionate heart.

Contents

Acknowledgements

My deepest thanks to:

My family and friends, who faithfully pray for me, tenderly comfort me, continually support me, consistently love me, graciously teach me and make me laugh every day. They are precious gifts from above.

My doctors and nurses, who gave me the best earthly care they possibly could and then watched as the Great Physician did the rest. They have always treated me with love and compassion. They shine within the medical community.

My church family, who welcomed me just as I was in 1991 and who have rejoiced with me, wept with me, prayed for me, taught me, encouraged me and loved me. What an inspiration they are.

My dear neighbor, Shelly, whose encouraging words set me on a path to discovering God's dream for me.

My publisher, Milt Adams, who helped turn God's dream for me into reality. What a mentor he has been.

My publisher's assistant, Judith, who has been so helpful to me. What a gift she is.

Jack Caravela at Mori Studio, whose design talent, attention to details, listening skills and kindness made the design process a joy to be involved in.

My editor, Shane Groth, who, as Milt said, "is so good at what he does!" I'm so thankful for his expertise!

My dear friends, Deb Mortimer, Linda Lehmann, Pearl Rader, Jill Mahoney, Kate Larsen, Kathie Kallevig and Nancy Kaysen, who God used mightily to encourage me in various aspects of the writing and publishing process.

Preface

My neighbor, Julie, recently gave me a book she had finished reading. While reading it one day, I came across these words uttered by one of the main characters, "Life can change with such shocking abruptness."

In 1991, at thirty-three years old, my own life changed "with such shocking abruptness" when I was diagnosed with stage four ovarian cancer. Overnight, my life became one of doctor appointments, medical tests, chemotherapy, hospital stays, and more. During that time, I endured physical, emotional and social changes. I also came face to face with my own immortality and didn't know whether my four-year-old son would have a mom in six months or not.

In that pit of despair, it became clear to me that I needed something to depend on; something that wouldn't change. So began my search. Eventually, I found what I was looking for. My spiritual eyes were opened, and I came to know the truth about God. My life again changed "with such shocking abruptness."

It is now 2003, twelve years after my life first changed "with such shocking abruptness." During the past twelve years, I have survived cancer three more times: a tumor wrapped around my sciatic nerve, colon cancer and breast cancer.

This book is a compilation of stories from my life during the past twelve years—stories that are "snapshots" of God at work in the crucible of cancer and ordinary daily life, stories that reveal God's love, grace, faithfulness and more. It is a book full of hope and inspiration.

Recently, I realized that my story is a lot like one of those 3D illusion pictures; the kind where if you look long and hard enough, another picture emerges. Some who look at my life "picture" or story will simply see cancer. But cancer is not the real story. Looking closer, you will find that the real story is about hope, miracles and God's amazing love. Join me as I share my *real* story . . .

Introduction
Life Before Cancer . . .
Before October 31, 1991

I was born in Minneapolis, Minnesota, on June 1, 1958, into a loving family that consisted of my dad, my mom and my brother, Randy, who was nine years old at the time. My parents had waited a long time for a second child, and so when I came along, I was truly loved and adored.

During my growing-up years, my dad was an accountant and my mom a housewife. Mom and Dad deeply loved each other, and they loved my brother and me. I was taught early on the importance of God, family and loving others. I was baptized as an infant and later confirmed. My parents read the Bible everyday, and we attended church together on Sundays. We even had family devotions during the week—devotions that were often cut short because of my giggling brought on by my brother's antics.

Nine years separated my brother and me, and there were times I felt like an only child. Unlike a lot of only children, though, I was never bored. I kept myself busy drawing, playing the guitar and playing with friends at the neighborhood creek at the "old shack" or "campsite." I also kept busy learning new crafts, like macramé and tatting, from one of our neighbors.

As I grew and became a teenager, I was very involved with our church youth group. I was always eager to sign up for the many retreats and projects available to us back then. Looking back, one of my favorite projects was recording songs we sang in our youth group. We then took a bus trip from Minneapolis to California and sold those recordings along the way.

Another teenage memory comes to mind. I remember someone asking me a question one day. I don't remember who asked it, where I was, or any of the other details, but I do remember the question: "If you happened to die tonight, would you go to heaven?" I still remember how that question haunted me. Although I was baptized, confirmed, went to church every Sunday, knew the ten commandments, agreed intellectually that Jesus was God's Son, and did good deeds when opportunities arose, I honestly couldn't say whether I would go to heaven. But even though that question haunted me, I never talked to anyone else about it. Instead, I tried not to think about it a whole lot and hoped that I would go to heaven.

When I was in high school, I was exposed to more and more people who used alcohol, something that was so foreign to me. My mom never drank and my dad only drank occasionally. I caved in under high school peer pressure and began experimenting with alcohol. Underage friends and I would occasionally go to the neighborhood bar on the weekends for fun. Once we became legal drinking age, those visits became a regular occurrence.

After high school, I went to the University of Minnesota, where I majored in Retail Merchandising. I fell in love with campus life, including weekend parties. While at the U of M,

I got an internship at a classic women's clothing store that was just opening up. At the time, it was a dream come true.

During the time of that internship, I met my husband Pete, and we were married a little over a year later in 1982. During the early years of our marriage, Pete and I both worked full-time. When the weekends came, we were always ready for a good time. Over time, though, it wasn't just the weekends that called for a good time. Our lives back then consisted of work and more and more parties.

In 1984, Pete got a job transfer to Dallas, Texas. It wasn't easy leaving Minneapolis and saying goodbye to lifelong friends and family. Just weeks before Christmas, though, Pete and I said our final goodbyes and headed south to our new home in the Lone Star state. Family and friends were left behind. And so was God.

Pete and I lived in Texas for a year and a half. Over the course of our stay there, we experienced both good times and bad times. But the bad times certainly outweighed the good. While we were living in Texas, my mom passed away back in Minnesota, I had a miscarriage, and following my miscarriage, Pete lost his job. We decided then that it was time to go back home—back to Minnesota.

In 1987, our son Zach was born. I quit working full-time and was anxious to be a stay-at-home mom. But as Pete began to travel every other week during that time, there were days I felt like a single parent. With a new baby and without a car, I began to feel trapped during the weeks Pete was on the road. I anxiously awaited the weekends—weekends which continued to include parties.

When Zach turned two years old, I took a part-time job at a clothing store. It was a time for me to get out of the house and to have real conversations with other adults. It was also a great time for Pete and Zach to bond even more. They always had fun stories to tell me of their time spent together while I was at work.

After I began working part-time, my creative talents began to surface again, and I began producing and selling some of my artwork at a few specialty stores and local craft fairs. It was at that time that I became obsessed with my artwork . . . constantly trying to come up with new ideas, new projects. Obsessed with my artwork, I didn't have time to think a lot about the growing sense of emptiness I had been feeling and the lack of true meaning and purpose in my life. During that time, my artwork served as an escape for me.

By then it was 1991, six months before my cancer diagnosis. It was late spring when I began experiencing side pain and indigestion. Every time I wore exercise leggings, the side pain would appear and wouldn't go away until I took the leggings off. Indigestion was the other symptom I experienced then, and I couldn't pinpoint the cause of it. Eventually, I made a doctor's appointment to get some answers.

At that first appointment, the doctor didn't have much to say about the indigestion I was experiencing. He told me the side pain was probably a pulled muscle, something I found hard to believe. I remember leaving that appointment with a gut feeling that the doctor was wrong . . . that it was more than just a simple pulled muscle.

Days later, I made an appointment to get a second opinion. During that appointment I mentioned that my mom had had ovarian cancer. "You're way too young for that," was the doctor's quick reply. I left that second appointment without any clear answers either.

For the next six months, I went from doctor to doctor, trying to figure out the true cause of my side pain and indigestion. During those months, I had gotten progressively worse, yet I still didn't have any answers. Brushed off by many doctors, I was even made to feel like a hypochondriac. I knew my body, though, and I knew something was definitely wrong.

At the end of those long and frustrating six months, I returned to my gynecologist. By then bloated and feeling even more miserable, I was very desperate for some answers and some relief.

During the appointment with my gynecologist, he decided to schedule a laparoscopy for me—a simple surgery wherein a small incision is made and a camera is inserted so the doctor can take a look around. He scheduled the laparoscopy for October 31, 1991. Unfortunately, that was the same day as the local craft fair I had been preparing for. All my hard work to get my artwork ready had been for nothing. But I was desperate, in need of answers and a whole lot more . . . I just didn't know it at the time.

Part One
(Ovarian Cancer)

Fear and the Diagnosis

For most people in Minneapolis, October 31, 1991, brings back memories of a record-breaking snowstorm, a snowstorm when Minneapolis was hit with more than twenty-eight inches of snow. For me, that date has a different memory . . . a simple surgery had been scheduled for me to find out why I had been experiencing side pain and indigestion for six months. I was told the surgery would take about an hour.

My family waited at the hospital while I was in surgery that day. They waited and waited, then waited some more. Finally, after six long hours in surgery, the surgeon appeared and talked with them. He did not have good news. In fact, it was shocking news. After he discussed the details of my surgery and diagnosis with my relatives, he came to my bedside. Still groggy from surgery, I heard the bad news myself: I had stage four ovarian cancer, they couldn't remove it all, I had to endure six months of intensive chemotherapy and, because they had done a hysterectomy, our hopes of having more children were gone. I was thirty-three years old. My life forever changed that day. It changed "with such

1

shocking abruptness." Years later, I can still picture my doctor leaning over the hospital bed, sharing that grim news with me. It seemed like a nightmare. I couldn't take it all in.

In the hospital the day after surgery, thoughts of my surgery and cancer diagnosis consumed my mind. At the same time, my emotions ricocheted from shock to sadness to fear. Haunting memories of my mom's own struggle with the same disease raced through my mind that day, too. Haunting memories that became a regular unwanted visitor of mine.

I was in the hospital for three weeks following surgery. While there, my doctor told me that I needed to concentrate on recovering from surgery so that I could start chemotherapy. Well, I did just that, and when visitors brought up my future treatments, I changed the subject. "First things first," I told myself. The truth of the matter was that the cancer diagnosis itself was just too much for me to take in at that point. In fact, it wasn't until weeks later that I could even say the words, "I have cancer."

During those hard days and long nights, I cried out to the God of my childhood Sunday school days. And during that time, I realized that I desperately needed something to hold onto—something that wouldn't change. And so began my search. A gift, a visit, and a sermon aided me in that search, and eventually I found what I was looking for . . .

A Gift, a Visit and a Sermon

We felt we were doomed to die and saw how powerless we were to help ourselves: but that was good, for then we put everything into the hands of God, who alone could save us, for he can even raise the dead. (2 Corinthians 1:9)

Cancer at age thirty-three had not been part of my plans for my life, and my mind had a hard time accepting the cold hard facts. In fact, it wasn't until weeks later that the reality of my diagnosis began to sink in and I could actually say the words, "I have cancer."

My chemotherapy treatments came every three weeks, and they were grueling. So grueling, in fact, that there were days I wanted to die. I couldn't believe it when others said to me, "You're lucky to be alive." At the time, I didn't feel lucky. I was in the deepest, darkest pit of my life and didn't know whether I would survive or not. Would my four-year-old son have a mom in six months? I didn't know. Face to face with death, I battled fear daily. But God was at work. He had a plan. An incredible, wonderful plan . . .

My friend, Deb, came to visit me in the hospital following my surgery. She came one night with a gift in hand. A gift I will never forget . . . a Bible. I hadn't read the Bible in years. But I discovered there was nothing like cancer to get you thinking about spiritual things. The timing of that gift was perfect.

In and out of the hospital, I began seeking God as one seeking a lost and valuable treasure . . . with urgency and commitment. I began praying more than ever, and I began reading the Bible Deb had given me. One day I remember saying, "I feel like my faith is the size of a pea." (It wasn't until later that I learned what Jesus said about faith the size of a mustard seed in Luke 17:6.)

As I sought God, I began to find Him, which is exactly what God promises in this verse I later discovered while reading the Bible: "You will find me when you seek me, if you look for me in earnest" (Jeremiah 29:13).

A month after I started chemotherapy, we moved into my in-laws' townhouse while they were in Florida. One night while we were eating, there was a knock at the door. Pete went to see who it was and returned with Don, the dad of my friend Deb. (The same Deb who had given me the Bible.)

Pete and I had met Don briefly when we lived in Texas but didn't really know him very well at all. Pete and I looked at each other, curious to know why Don had stopped by and why he had his Bible with him.

During the course of our conversation that night, Don asked us what the main message of the Bible was. Pete and I both answered, "Love." Even though our Bible knowledge was limited, we remembered that fact from our Sunday school days as children.

The idea of God's love hit me so differently the night of Don's visit. I could tangibly feel God's love surrounding us— like a down comforter on a cold winter's night. Don left us with food for thought that night and then showed up again the next night . . . and the next night and the next night. He didn't push anything on us but talked of God's love.

After nights of Don's visits, Pete and I decided to read the Bible together, something we had never done before. We didn't know where to start, but on a Saturday night, we just opened it and began to read. Matthew 8:1–4 is where we began reading. It's the story of Jesus healing a leper.

Deb and Don had invited us to their church the next day. Desperate and willing to try anything, Pete and I accepted their invitation without giving it a second thought.

At church the next day, Pete dropped Zach and me off at the door before parking the car. Zach and I entered the church and sat near the back so that Pete could easily spot us among the large crowd gathered there.

Before Pete arrived, I read the program and noticed that the scripture for that Sunday was Matthew 8:1–4—the same story we had read the night before! I sensed then that it wasn't a coincidence. It was more than that. I knew that something indescribable was definitely happening.

The pastor talked about leprosy in his sermon, and likened it to today's dreaded diseases of cancer and AIDS. Through that sermon, I heard God speak to me like never before. That morning, the sermon reached my heart, not just my head. And I was convinced after hearing it, that I, like the leper, had to go to Jesus. I first had to worship Him, ask to be healed, believe that He could heal me, but also understand that He may choose not to. The words of that sermon stayed with me.

As I continued to seek God, He continued revealing Himself to me through prayer, the Bible, and other Christians. Then, amazingly, He chose to reveal Himself to me through a broom and a song . . .

A Broom and a Song

I shall not die but live to tell of all his deeds.
(Psalm 118:17)

At first I didn't know what to make of this regular occurrence in my life. At the time I didn't know what to call it. I now know that it was a vision from God. Here's what happened . . .

One night shortly after beginning my chemotherapy treatments for ovarian cancer, I was trying to fall asleep. Chemotherapy had wreaked havoc on my sleep schedule, and I was experiencing many sleepless nights. On that particular night, I remember being almost asleep, when all of a sudden, a picture of Jesus popped up on the screen of my mind. As I fully concentrated on Him, I noticed something unusual. Jesus was sweeping.

As a child, I had seen pictures of Jesus knocking on a door, healing the sick, hanging on the cross, but never ever sweeping. I was struck by how very unusual that picture in my mind truly was.

As I watched Jesus sweeping in my mind, a song came to me then, too. It was a song I had sung many years before in my church youth group: "I am the Good Shepherd, come and follow me. I am the Good Shepherd, come and follow me." That song from my past played over and over in my mind. Although I didn't understand the meaning of all that was going on in my mind, I was comforted and soon fell asleep. The next morning, I woke up and remembered Jesus sweeping and the song that had been playing in my mind. I thought about it a lot that day and the following days. I decided not to tell anyone else about it, though, because they might think I was crazy.

That same experience of seeing Jesus sweeping and hearing the song in my mind began happening to me on a regular basis. Eventually, I decided that I had to tell someone about it. I finally decided that my friend Deb was the one I could tell. I trusted her completely and thought she might have some insight regarding it.

One day, I mustered up enough courage to tell Deb. After hearing the details about what had been playing in my mind, Deb was clearly excited. As her excitement traveled through the phone line, Deb told me she thought it was a sign. A sign from above that Jesus was sweeping the cancer out of my body; that He was going to heal me. Considering Deb's response, I was excited, too.

After Deb told her dad, Don, about my experience, Don made a standup figure of Jesus sweeping, with a tiny hand-made broom. He told me to bring the cutout of Jesus to the hospital when I had chemotherapy and to place it near the bed where I could see it. Well, I did just that, and every time I spotted that figure, it reminded me that Jesus was near and that He *was* sweeping the cancer out of my body. For I, like Deb, had also come to believe that the picture of Jesus sweeping in my mind truly was a sign; a promise from God that He was going to heal me.

I clung to that sign as God's promise to me, even when the days were dark and filled with despair. I chose to believe

God. I chose to trust Him, even though my circumstances begged me to abandon that trust.

In Isaiah 14:23 the Lord says He "will sweep the land [of Babylon] with the broom of *destruction*." One day at a time, I was being swept clean physically, by God's broom of *grace*. Eventually, I was swept clean spiritually . . . one day in a hospital room . . . undergoing chemotherapy . . .

Found at Last!

Something that wouldn't change, something that I could depend on . . .

I was undergoing another difficult therapy treatment in January of 1991, when I found what I had been searching for . . . something that wouldn't change; something I could always depend on . . .

It started out like any other day. Any other day in the hospital, that is. Awake at the crack of dawn, breakfast in bed(!), medical staff coming and going, shower time, lab work, medical tests and more. Then lunch—something I rarely had an appetite for during those days of chemotherapy. Trying to eat lunch that particular day, I had no idea what I was about to discover that afternoon.

After lunch, alone and lying in bed, the words of a song came to me: "Turn your eyes upon Jesus, look full in His wonderful face, and the things of earth will grow strangely dim, in the light of His glory and grace." I was pondering those words when suddenly my spiritual eyes were opened, and for the first time in my life I understood who Jesus really was. He was the One who, at the cross, paid in full the penalty for my sins; my raggedness. I realized then that receiving eternal life wasn't about me being good enough or about me earning my way to heaven through good deeds, church attendance, and so on, but rather it was about Jesus Christ and what He had already done for me.

That afternoon, I also realized that it wasn't only others who had hidden motives, or others who had gossiped, lied, judged others, lusted and more, but that I, too, was guilty. That day, I saw myself according to God's perfect standards instead of the world's standards. And with my sins stacked up against me, I recognized my own need for a Savior.

So there, alone in my hospital room, I confessed my sins and asked Jesus into my heart to be my Savior and Lord. I finally wanted to follow the Good Shepherd, just like the song on my mind had instructed me: "I am the Good Shepherd, *come and follow me,* I am the Good Shepherd, *come and follow me."*

After asking Jesus to be my Savior and Lord, no more doubts remained regarding my eternal destiny. It was then I knew for sure that my heavenly reservation was guaranteed. There in my hospital room, an overwhelming sense of peace and joy that I had never known before flooded my heart. I felt as if a huge burden had been lifted from my shoulders. I also knew then that I had finally found what I had been searching for. Jesus was that "something" that wouldn't change, the One that I could always depend on—even when my world was turned upside down.

Lying in my hospital bed, I considered what was still ahead of me; more chemotherapy treatments, probably more horrible side effects, probably more scary tests, probably more hard days and long nights. Yet the overwhelming peace I was experiencing remained. For I knew then without a shadow of a doubt, that Jesus . . . who had walked on water, given sight to the blind, healed the lame, turned water into wine, and more, would see me through. Jesus would *always* see me through, one day at a time.

Days and weeks later, my mind returned over and over to that day in the hospital when I asked Jesus into my heart— the day my spiritual eyes were opened and my spiritual life began. I marveled at God's amazing grace and thanked Him over and over for sending Jesus to die for our sins—for my sins, and for loving me that much. With Jesus in my heart, I was a new creation, just like 2 Corinthians 5:17 tells us. And unbelievable changes began to occur in my life. For life with Jesus always brings change. Every single time . . .

A New Life

Therefore, if anyone is in Christ, he is a new creation; the old has gone, the new has come! (2 Corinthians 5:17, NIV)

My life before Jesus and after Jesus is like night and day to me. With Jesus in my heart, unbelievable changes began to occur, changes that were like bright shining stars in the dark night of cancer I was enduring.

After asking Jesus into my heart, I was a new creation, and I have truly felt like a new creation, with new eyes, a new heart, new desires and a new eternal destiny.

My new eyes began to see things from a whole new perspective. I began to see things from God's perspective and not my own limited earthly one. My new eyes began to recognize God's hand on my life and to see spiritual lessons in my daily life. My new heart began to overflow with God's love and compassion for others, a kind of love that I could never muster up on my own. My new heart was full of thanks for God's blessings and tender mercies in my life, and peace began reigning where fear had once ruled.

My new desires were God's desires for me. No longer a slave to sin and my old selfish desires—like when I was obsessed with art—I desired to go God's way and to know His plans for my life. My old desires to party disappeared, and I desired to really know God through reading the Bible and through prayer.

My new eternal destiny filled me with incredible hope and took away my fear of death. I discovered back then that a heavenly reservation has a way of doing that . . .

My relationship with Jesus began to affect every part of my life: how I spent my time and money, how I used the talents I had been given. My relationship with Christ began to affect my attitudes, my thoughts, and my words as well. It also affected my relationships with others, how I took care of my body, even what movies and TV shows I watched and what books and magazines I read. My relationship with Jesus also affected my life's focus. Instead of focusing on things that had no eternal value, I began focusing on things of eternal value—like Bible study, prayer, loving others, and doing the things God was calling me to do.

My relationship with Jesus also affected how I made decisions. I began going to God and the Bible for guidance and wisdom. I learned that because God is all-knowing and is also my creator, He knows what's best for me at all times. He wants me to depend on Him. He knows the way, and nothing is impossible with Him. One day, I realized that it was my own pride that used to tell me I could handle things on my own and didn't need to depend on anyone . . . not even God.

I also began to pray about everything, not just crisis situations. Anytime. Anywhere. I discovered then that the phone line to Heaven is never busy . . .

With Jesus in my heart, I also began reading the Bible more and more. It was unbelievable to me that I was actually reading the Bible! Me, the former party girl. Wow! Talk about change! The Bible became an important part of my everyday life, and I learned the importance of knowing God's word for good times and for bad.

Looking back, I saw that for most of my life I had experienced "religion." "Religion" that had left me feeling empty, fearful and cold. Thankfully, I learned that it's not about "religion," but rather about a relationship. Religion could have never changed my heart, for only a relationship with Jesus can do that. Changing hearts is Jesus' specialty. I'm living proof of that.

Day by day, slowly but surely, my heart continues to change, and I am being transformed into the image of Jesus (God's goal for all believers). Believe me, I have a long way to go. I'm not perfect yet. But God is, and He's still at work. And like Philippians 1:6(NIV) tells us, "He who began a good work in (me) will carry it on to completion until the day of Christ Jesus."

Hope

For I know the plans I have for you," declares the Lord, "plans to prosper you and not to harm you, plans to give you hope and a future. (Jeremiah 29:11, NIV)

Lord, when doubts fill my mind, when my heart is in turmoil, quiet me and give me renewed hope and cheer. (Psalm 94:19)

I had recently started chemotherapy treatments for ovarian cancer when Pete had to go out of town on business for a night. He was headed to Des Moines, Iowa, and Zach and I headed to my in-laws' for the night. It was a stormy winter night, and I felt miserable from my chemo treatments. All I had wanted to do was to stay home, cozy in my bed. But, realistically, I knew I needed help taking care of Zach, who was four years old at that time.

Shortly after Pete dropped us off at his parents' townhouse, he called from the airport. His flight to Des Moines had been postponed because of the snowstorm that evening. Pete also told me he'd keep me informed about his situation. He called again later and told me that he and his boss were going to take a puddle jumper to Des Moines. "Yikes! In a snowstorm?" I quietly asked myself. I told him I didn't want him to go, but he said they had to go. I hung up the phone and grew more tense with each passing minute. Thoughts of

Pete and his boss bouncing around at night in a small plane during a raging snowstorm crowded out any other thoughts in my brain—and the more worried I became. Eventually, I was consumed with fear.

What if they crashed? What if I didn't survive cancer? What would happen to Zach? What if? What if? What if?

Zach and my in-laws were in another room, unaware of my thoughts and consuming fears at that moment. I felt so alone and so scared. Tears welled up in my eyes, and I silently cried out to God.

After crying out to God, I spotted my Bible, the gift from my friend Deb. For some reason, I had brought it along to my in-laws' that night. In desperation, I grabbed that Bible and quickly opened it, landing on Psalm 116. I read, *"I love the Lord because He hears my prayers and answers them. Because He bends down and listens, I will pray as long as I breathe!"* Death stared me in the face—I was frightened and sad. Then I cried, 'Lord, save me!' How kind He is! How good He is! So merciful, this God of ours! The Lord protects the simple and the childlike; I was facing death and then He saved me. Now I can relax. For the Lord has done this wonderful miracle for me. He has saved me from death, my eyes from tears, my feet from stumbling. *I shall live! Yes, in His presence—here on earth!* In my discouragement I thought, 'They are lying when they say I will recover.' But now what can I offer Jehovah for all He has done for me? I will bring Him an offering of wine and praise His name for saving me. I will publicly bring Him the sacrifice I vowed I would. *His loved ones are very precious to Him and He does not lightly let them die.* Oh Lord, you have freed me from my bonds and I will serve you forever. I will worship you and offer you a sacrifice of thanksgiving. Here in the courts of the Temple in Jerusalem, before all the people, I will pay everything I vowed to the Lord. Praise the Lord." (verse 1–19, my emphasis)

I read Psalm 116 once and then again. I was amazed! It was as if Psalm 116 had been written especially for me; for my situation. Verses 1, 2, 9, and 15 (italicized verses) stood out to me, and I was somehow comforted. At the time, I didn't understand how.

After reading Psalm 116 several more times, my fears lessened even more and I called my friend Deb to tell her about my circumstances and my reading. Deb grabbed her own Bible and after reading Psalm 116 herself, told me she believed it was another sign from God that He was going to heal me. I felt her joyous excitement over the phone line and I got excited, too. Excited and less fearful still.

Even though I wasn't a Christian that stormy winter night at my in-laws', I now see that I was seeking God by turning to the Bible. And God in His great and tender mercy had drawn near to comfort me through Psalm 116. God's Word gave me the strength I needed to make it through that stormy night.

Looking back, I realize that there were two storms going on that night. One was a blinding snowstorm outside my in-laws' townhouse and the other was a raging storm of fear within my soul. One storm was physical, the other spiritual. And the One who allowed the raging snowstorm outside the window was the same One who stilled the raging storm inside my soul. He stilled my soul through His Word . . .

That night, God's Word was like a lighthouse to get me safely through the storm. It guided me to a place of comfort and hope, away from the crashing waves of fear. It gave me hope in the night.

God's Word continues to comfort me and give me hope in the night. Regardless of the storm I may be enduring—inside or out.

P.S. Psalm 116:9 ("I shall live! Yes, in His presence—here on earth!") stayed with me for days and weeks following that snowstorm. It wasn't until I received Christ several weeks later that I, like Deb, became convinced that Psalm 116:9 was God's promise to me—another sign He was going to heal me. And during the times my mind silently questioned whether I was going to survive or not, God would gently bring those comforting words of Psalm 116 to mind again.

The Best Advice in the Worst of Times

Hallelujah! Yes, praise the Lord! Praise Him in His Temple, and in the heavens He made with mighty power. Praise Him for His mighty works. Praise His unequaled greatness. Praise Him with the trumpet and with lute and harp. Praise Him with the tambourines and processional. Praise Him with stringed instruments and horns. Praise Him with the cymbals, yes, loud clanging cymbals. Let everything alive give praises to the Lord! You praise Him! Hallelujah!
(Psalm 150)

It's just human nature to offer others advice—in good times and in bad. But in my experience, it's the bad times that solicit the most advice from others. During my ovarian cancer, I received all kinds of advice. My head swam with advice from doctors, nurses, family and friends who were all trying to help. Of all the advice I received back then, though, one bit of advice still stands out in my mind to this day. It is one of the best bits of advice I have ever received, and it came to me from Don, my friend Deb's dad. Don's advice to me one day was straightforward and simple—"Praise God!" he told me. And then after sharing his advice with me, Don passed along an article titled, "Praise Transforms."

At first I thought Don was crazy. Praise God in the midst of the most trying time of my life? Praise God when I was sicker than sick and weaker than weak? What was Don thinking? I wondered.

I was desperate back then. I felt like I was hanging on by a thin thread and I was willing to try just about anything that might help. The article from Don stated that, out of praise came faith, courage, optimism, strength, clarity, peace, health, happiness and soul satisfaction. It also noted that nothing delights the Father's heart as much as the praises of His children. After reading the article and pondering Don's words to me, I realized I had nothing to lose. So one day I began to praise God . . . for His love, His faithfulness and more. Not that I *felt* like praising God, but I *chose* to praise Him. Amazingly, as I praised God that day, I was changed. Somehow, my load was lightened and my attitude brightened. Yes! Praise transforms! I don't know how, but I learned that day that it truly does.

Since that first day of praising God, I have learned that the more I praise God, the more I *feel* like praising God. I have also learned that praising God is an essential ingredient of the Christian life, and when my spiritual life seems flat, lack of praise is usually the culprit.

Since the time I took Don's advice to heart, I have tried to live a life of praise. I have found that I can praise God anywhere, anytime. I can praise Him at work, rest or play. I can praise Him through words or through songs, I can praise Him silently or out loud. I can praise Him by myself or together with a group.

Praise comes easiest when the way is easy. But I must continue to praise God—*choose* to praise God—no matter what my circumstances are. I am so thankful for Don's straightforward and simple, yet bold, advice to me. At a time, I later realized, I needed it most. Like the doxology song proclaims, "Praise God from whom all blessings flow." I continue to praise Him always, for His blessings always flow. In good times and in bad . . .

Baby Steps

He who belongs to God hears what God says (John 8:47, NIV).

The steps of good men are directed by the Lord. He delights in each step they take. (Psalm 37:23).

In his heart a man plans his course, but the Lord determines his steps (Proverbs 16:9, NIV).

No matter how old Zach gets, I think I will always remember his "firsts" as a baby. His first word, his first haircut, his first tooth, his first birthday, and of course his first baby steps.

Although all a baby's firsts are important, nothing quite compares to the day a baby takes those first steps. As parents, we anxiously anticipate them, and our hearts leap with joy when our baby finally does walk.

As I think about Zach's first baby steps, I'm reminded of my steps as a baby Christian. And just like I can clearly remember Zach's first baby steps, so I can clearly remember my first steps—specifically, my first steps on the road of recognizing God's voice in my life.

At the time, I was undergoing chemotherapy and was suffering daily debilitating side effects from it. I was physically unable to take care of Zach and myself. So my dear friend Leslie, whom I've known since fifth grade and is more like a sister to me than a friend, offered to help. More than once a week, Leslie picked up Zach and me, drove us to her home and lovingly took care of us (along with her three kids!) while Pete was at work.

Every time we hung out at Leslie's during those long months of chemotherapy, I would rest in the afternoon after lunch. One day, while lying down, a Bible verse came to me. "But they that wait upon the Lord shall renew their strength. They shall mount up with wings like eagles; they shall run and not be weary; they shall walk and not faint" (Isaiah 40:31). I was so physically weak back then that when Isaiah 40:31 came to me, I was greatly comforted.

From that day forward, Isaiah 40:31 began coming to my mind on a regular basis—usually when I was resting at Leslie and her husband Mark's house, but at other times, too. Like the day I went for a walk around the block with my dad for example. After Dad and I had walked only one block, I felt like fainting. Discouraged, I turned around and went back to his house. On my walk back, Isaiah 40:31 came to mind again, and I was again comforted.

Then came the day I'll never forget. Lying on Leslie and Mark's bed one afternoon, Isaiah 40:31 came to me again. But on that particular day, my spiritual eyes were opened, and I realized that God was personally speaking to me through it. As a new Christian, I had heard that God speaks to us through the Bible, His Word, but that afternoon was the first time I actually recognized God's voice through His Word— on my own—without the added insight of other believers. That day was the day of my first baby steps on the road to recognizing God's voice in my life. It was truly incredible. I was amazed that the God of the Universe was talking to ME through His word! Isaiah 40:31 became the verse I hung onto at the time because I knew it had been sent special delivery from God to me. Eventually, I believed what God was actually telling me through it, too. I began to believe that if I waited on God, He *would* renew my strength, that I *would* mount up with wings like eagle's, that I *would* run and not be weary, and that someday I *would* walk and not faint, even if the walk was more than a block.

Pondering those baby steps on my Christian walk anew, I realize that the process of Zach learning to walk is a perfect analogy to my learning to walk on the road of recognizing God's voice in my life.

First, I recall how I anxiously anticipated Zach's first steps, and I imagine how God, my Heavenly Father, must have anticipated my first steps back then, waiting and watching from heaven's window. Second, I remember "cheering" Zach on. I couldn't wait until he walked into my waiting arms. I pictured how God must have cheered me on, too, holding out his "everlasting arms." Third, I remember how Zach hung onto the furniture before he launched out on his own. I, too, hung on—not to furniture, but to the added insight of others before I finally recognized God's voice on my own. Fourth, I remember Zach's determination when learning to walk. He'd take a few steps, fall down and then get right back up to try again. After I recognized God's voice speaking to me through Isaiah 40:31, I, too, was determined. I wanted to hear from my Heavenly Father again and again. So I earnestly sought Him through His Word and prayer. Fifth, I remember how shaky Zach's first steps were after he let go of the furniture. It took awhile before his steps were sure. I, too, was "shaky" at first, not always sure of God's voice. But over time, just as Zach's steps became sure, mine have, too. With God's help, I have come to recognize His voice in my life and to know it without a doubt. But even though my steps have become sure, I continue and must *always* continue to hold onto my Heavenly Father's hand.

Learning to walk is a process, and although Zach learned to walk physically as a baby, I am still learning to walk spiritually. God has taught me well how to walk on the road of recognizing His voice, but there are other roads on which I am still learning how to walk. Other roads like the road of love, the road of contentment, the road of serving others and more. Thinking of steps, I'm reminded of the words from a song by Beker called "Step by Step."

The words of that song echo the cry of my heart. Daily, I want to praise God, to seek Him in the morning, to learn to walk in His ways and to follow Him wherever He leads. For He knows the way. And if I take His hand each day and step out in faith, He will lead me home, one step . . . one *baby* step . . . at a time.

My Guardian Angel

And now Christ is in heaven sitting in the place of honor next to God the Father, with all the angels and powers of heaven bowing before Him and obeying Him. (1 Peter 3:22)

The highest of angelic powers stand in dread and awe of Him. Who is as revered as He by those surrounding Him? (Psalm 89:7)

No, for the angels are only spirit messengers sent out to help and care for those who are to receive His salvation. (Hebrews 1:14)

God speaks of His angels as messengers swift as the wind and as servants made of flaming fire. (Hebrews 1:7)

Don't forget to be kind to strangers for some who have done this have entertained angels without realizing it. (Hebrews 13:2)

*Don't let anyone declare you lost when you
refuse to worship angels, as they say you must.
They have seen a vision, they say, and know you
should. These proud men (though they claim to
be so humble) have a very clever imagination.
But they are not connected to Christ, the Head
to which all of us who are His body are joined;
for we are joined together by His strong sinews,
and we grow only as we get our nourishment
and strength from God. (Colossians 2:18,19)*

It's now 2001, and the angel craze continues. Angel movies,
angel TV shows, angel books, angel pictures and a myriad of
angel knick-knacks. For some, I believe, an interest in angels
may be a stepping-stone to learning the truth about Jesus
Christ. For others, though, I fear their fascination with angels
may result in their worshipping angels instead of the living
God, something Colossians 2:18 clearly warns against.

As I think about the angel craze going on around me, I
am reminded of Alan, the one I nicknamed "my guardian
angel" years ago.

Of all the people we meet during our lives there are probably only a handful who will forever hold an extra special
place in our hearts. Alan is one of those.

My family's friendship with Alan began in 1991 when I
was in the hospital recovering from major surgery for ovarian
cancer. Back then, the hospital scene was so foreign to me,
and I personally found it to be very unnerving. It seemed
there was a constant stream of hospital staff going in and out
of my room at all hours of the day or night. And when the

staff entered my room, I never knew exactly what was in store for me . . . more blood work, more tests or more bad news?

One day in particular during that time stands out vividly in my mind, the day I met Alan. Alan, one of the hospital staff from the X-ray department, entered my room and told me he was going to take me downstairs for a CT scan. My mind raced and my hands began to sweat as Alan spoke those words. I was then left alone with my fears as Alan went to find someone to help him get me onto a cart so he could bring me downstairs for the test. Alan returned shortly with help and soon wheeled me down the hall to the elevator. Lying on the cart, I was paralyzed with fear. For at the time, I hadn't personally met Jesus Christ yet, and I was dealing with my fears alone. I felt no peace whatsoever.

Waiting for the elevator, Alan sensed my fear. He looked at me with eyes full of concern and compassion and asked me what was wrong. I told him that I was extremely claustrophobic and was scared to death to go into an enclosed body tube for the scan. Alan was quick to point out to me that I was thinking of the MRI test and not a CT scan. With the CT scan, I would not be fully enclosed and I had nothing to worry about. Aahh . . . relief. My fears instantly melted away, and I was so thankful for Alan that day.

After that CT scan, Alan became one of my regular visitors every time I was in the hospital. Whenever I needed encouragement, Alan would amazingly show up. His compassion, sense of humor and his gentle words of wisdom always encouraged me and helped to ease my burden.

I wasn't the only one in the family who was encouraged by Alan, either. Pete and Dad were also blessed by their interactions with him. They, too, became friends with him.

I can still picture the day when Pete went down to the hospital coffee shop for a break. Upon returning to my room, he excitedly told me that he had run into Alan. At first this didn't seem unusual to me, until I remembered that Alan worked nights, not days. After talking to Alan for a while that day in the coffee shop, Pete was encouraged, and his face clearly revealed it when he returned to my room.

Alan greatly encouraged Dad, too, and not only during his hospital visits to me. Years later, when Dad himself was hospitalized, Alan stopped by to visit him, too. I can still picture Dad's eyes lighting up when he told me that Alan had stopped by.

It's been years since the day I first met Alan, but I con-tinue to refer to him as my "guardian angel"—an endearing nickname for one who encouraged me, calmed my fears, took the time to listen and took the time to care, time and time again.

Hebrews 1:14 says, "Angels are only spirit messengers sent out to help and care for those who are to receive His salvation." Is Alan really one of God's angels? Probably not, although at times I really have wondered. But, like an angel, Alan *was* a messenger; a messenger of hope and love sent to us by God—in His perfect timing.

I am still so very thankful for Alan, "my guardian angel," the one who has deeply touched our lives. My prayer is that I, like Alan, will be a messenger of hope and love to those hurting around me and that I will always point them to the true comforter of all, Jesus Christ. He is the One we can always depend on . . . the One who never changes . . . the One who became far greater than the angels . . . the One who even the angels worship and adore. That is a thought worth meditating on in the angel-crazed world in which I live. And when I do meditate on that thought, I'm reminded of the words I sang as a child during Sunday school, "Holy, Holy, Holy! All the saints adore thee, casting down their golden crowns around the glassy sea, cherubim and seraphim falling down before thee, which wert and art, and evermore shall be. Amen."

May we, like the angels, worship and adore Him . . . fall down before Him.

Robbie

I weep with grief; my heart is heavy with sorrow; encourage and cheer me with your words. (Psalm 119:28)

We had just gotten home from our family's annual Christmas cookie bake and I was exhausted, so I lay down to rest for a while. A few minutes later, the phone rang. "T, I've got some bad news," my dear friend Leslie said.

It was horrible news, awful news. I couldn't believe what Leslie was telling me about Robbie, one of our neighbors during our growing-up years. Robbie was dead. He had been killed in Africa that week when a truck ran into the sightseeing bus he was on. Robbie was twenty-five years old at the time of the accident.

Memories of Robbie flashed through my mind as Leslie

spoke. I pictured Robbie walking around eating his "oweo" cookies (as he called them) while I babysat him. I also remembered how Robbie had gotten into everything when he was little . . . especially our hearts.

As the reality of the crushing news sunk in, a flood of tears coursed down my face. I cried uncontrollably. After my conversation with Leslie that night, I called Tom and Judy, Robbie's parents, to offer my condolences wrapped in tears. After that tearful conversation with them, I decided to get ready for bed. I slipped my pajamas on and climbed into bed, still teary-eyed and shaking. I prayed and reached for my Bible, hoping to find comfort there. But as I read, nothing spoke to me personally. So I closed my Bible and reached over to place it on the nightstand. As I did, a slip of paper fell out. I picked it up and discovered that it was a note in my own handwriting that simply said, Psalm 55:22. I didn't recall when I had written that note or why, but I quickly opened my Bible again and turned to the verse. "Cast your burden on the Lord, and He will sustain you; He will never permit the righteous to be moved" (NRSV).

After reading that passage, I was speechless. Those words were *exactly* what I needed to read at that moment. I read them over and over again. Eventually, I closed the Bible and then my eyes, hoping to sleep. But Psalm 55:22 continued to play in my mind. As it did, I felt God's peace and strength take over my despairing soul, and I was comforted. God's Word had reached my heart.

It was then that God inspired me with this song based on Psalm 55:22: *What do we do when sadness fills our hearts and tears us all apart? What can we do? What can we say to ease the pain of another? How can we make it through the night? Cast your burden upon the Lord, and He will sustain us. He will give us the peace that we need. He'll never leave us, He won't forsake us. He will give us the peace that we need. Cast your burden upon the Lord, and He will sustain us. Now and forever, cast your burden upon the Lord.*

Since the night I learned of Robbie's death, I've thought of Psalm 55:22 many times. It has continued to strengthen me and instruct me during many other dark and stormy nights. It always reminds me of what I need to do—"Cast (my) burden on the Lord," and then what promises I can claim—"He will sustain (me): He will never permit the righteous to be moved."

Through experience, I have learned that whenever I truly cast my burden on Him (by His grace), I reel in His *peace*, His *strength* and His *joy*. And when my net of troubles is transformed by that heavenly catch, I am sustained, comforted and able to go on. "Cast your burden on the Lord, and He will sustain you; He will never permit the righteous to be moved."

His Amazing Ways

I will seek my lost ones, those who have strayed away, and bring them safely home again. I will put splints and bandages upon their broken limbs and heal the sick. (Ezekiel 34:15)

Shortly before my ovarian cancer in 1991, there was a TV show called "Thirty Something" that revolved around a group of friends who were in their thirties, the same age Pete and I were at that time. Every week, I anxiously tuned into that show and watched as the characters shared the joys and sorrows of their everyday lives.

Months before my own cancer diagnosis, Nancy, my favorite character on the show, was diagnosed with ovarian cancer. Over several episodes, Nancy was shown going through the rigors of chemotherapy. I remembered thinking at that time what a great job both the writers and actress had done of portraying the reality of cancer as memories of my mom's own struggle with the same disease surfaced while watching those episodes.

Eventually, Nancy finished her chemotherapy treatments and survived the ovarian cancer. Nancy's story had a happy ending.

Months later, my own ovarian cancer diagnosis came at thirty-three years old. My mind returned many times to Nancy's struggle with cancer. I remembered her hospital visits, her hair loss, her sadness, her weight loss, her anxiety, and the strain on her marriage caused by cancer.

After starting chemotherapy treatments I lost a lot of weight. One day during that time, while looking at my skinny self in the mirror, I recalled a specific episode where Nancy's treatments had also caused weight loss. I remembered how Nancy had looked in the mirror one day, saw herself swimming in her too-large clothes and called herself "the incredible shrinking woman." I had become the "incredible shrinking woman" myself.

Although Nancy's struggle wasn't actually real life, somehow the memories of her struggle with ovarian cancer served as a shock absorber when the reality of my own diagnosis hit home. Those same memories also encouraged me time and again to continue on in the midst of my own intense chemotherapy.

His Amazing Ways: The Song

The summer before I had ovarian cancer, Pete, Zach and I lived in a condo and had weekly barbeques with our neighbors, Dave and Jackie. Whether poolside or on the knoll outside our condos, those weekly barbeques always included good food, beer and music. Pete was the one who usually took charge of the music back then, and that particular summer he had fallen in love with a new recording by one of his favorite singers. There was one song on that recording that quickly became a favorite of ours, and we sang it over and over again that summer, even when there wasn't a barbeque going on. We were simply drawn to that song. The name of the song was "Whenever God Shines His Light on Me" by Van Morrison.

The lyrics of that song talk about reaching out to God in confusion and despair, the fact that God will be there when we do, that we can share our troubles with God, that He heals the sick and lame, that we, too, can heal in Jesus' name, and that God will lift us up, turn us around and put our feet on higher ground.

After that summer of barbeques and singing "our" song, fall came, bringing with it my ovarian cancer diagnosis. That favorite summer song of ours continued to play in my mind. In fact, to gain my strength back after surgery I walked around and around our condo. As I did, I sang that song out loud. Day after day, night after night, it greatly encouraged me. I was especially drawn to the line that spoke of God healing the sick.

God's ways are truly amazing, but without spiritual eyesight, they are unrecognizable as such. At the time of my original diagnosis, I thought it was merely a coincidence that I had gotten ovarian cancer just like my favorite TV character Nancy had. And I thought that our new favorite song that summer was just a really good song and nothing more. But then after I asked Jesus into my heart and my spiritual eyes were opened, I gained a new perspective. I went from not seeing God at work in my life at all to seeing Him at work all around me . . . even through a TV show and a song.

God met me where I was as an unbeliever, and He took what was already in my life, a TV show and a song, and used them to accomplish His purposes in His perfect timing.

I truly believe God used that TV show with Nancy's ovarian cancer to prepare me for my own shocking cancer diagnosis months later. And He used the song to draw me to Himself and to reveal that He does heal the sick.

Remembering the TV show and song, I wonder what specific things in my life right now God may be using as preparation for things to come. I also wonder what things God may be using in my life today to draw me to Himself.

Looking back at that TV show and song, I am also encouraged. Encouraged because I'm reminded that God is sovereign and that He's not limited to just the Bible, the church or Christian literature in reaching the lost. For God can use anything to speak to anyone when drawing a person to Himself. Isn't that encouraging to remember? Isn't that incredible? But it certainly is nothing new. I think about other signs and remember the burning bush (Exodus 3) and the star o'er Bethlehem (Matthew 2) . . .

Poems I wrote to our four-year-old son, Zach, during cancer #1 . . .

Dear Zach,

My precious little one, my heart goes out to you,

For other kids your age rarely see the things you do.

But life isn't always easy or goes the way we planned,

So live each day to the fullest and love all that you can.

And remember Jesus loves us and will keep us in His care,

When our hearts are sad and breaking,

He will always be right there.

And although right now Mom's legs

won't let her run around the park,

We still can dance and sing and tell stories in the dark.

My love, I pray, will always keep you warm

when you are cold,

Wrap you like a blanket, as you keep growing old.

You fill my heart with laughter, my life with joy,

Oh, I'm so very lucky* that you're my little boy.

Love,

Mommy

---

*Years later I would use the word" blessed." I don't believe in luck anymore . . .

"B"

"B" was a gift when you were born,

So you see why he's a bit tattered and torn.

"B" is your bunny, and he's so much fun,

You named him yourself when you were just one.

"B's coming with," you'd insist all the time,

And so when he got full of dirt and grime,

We'd put him in the washer and you'd stand by,

You didn't like him in there—it made you cry.

But "B's" gotten older and so have you,

And "B" doesn't do all the things he used to.

But when it gets dark and we turn out the light

"B's" still at your side all through the night.

Dancing snowflakes

The snowflakes were dancing and tickling our noses,

Which the cold wind was painting the color of roses.

But our laughter kept us warm,

Really cozy through and through,

As we took a walk,

Just me and you.

Memories

When you were one you had so much fun,

Playing with our neighbor Jonathan.

You with your "B" and him with his thumb,

You'd run and laugh and play in the sun.

Oh, I never wanted those summer days to end.

But time just flew and then you were two,

And, oh, the things that you could do,

Like the alphabet, peek-a-boo

and reading books like *Winnie the Pooh*.

Oh, the soles of my shoes would never be the same.

Then you were three and were busy as can be,

"Mowing and trimming" around the trees,

And collecting things like rocks and keys.

I couldn't believe how fast the time had gone.

Now that you're four, it's bugs you adore.

Along with wrestling and playing with Dad on the floor.

You give us kisses and so much more.

What memories we have to store,

Forever in our hearts.

For babies don't stay babies,

They grow up, oh, so fast,

Thank goodness for pictures and memories that last.

Tank to me (Thank you me)

Cookies were "tooties" for quite a long while,

and good was "dood"; your words made me smile.

You mixed up your Cs and your Ts and your Gs,

"Tank to me" is what you said

when you got what you pleased.

You had your own language as most children do,

and Mommy would translate as most mommies do.

But "tooties" became cookies and "dood" became good

and you started to say words as you should.

Daddy was relieved and mommy was sad.

For the baby she once knew,

She no longer had.

Sweet Dreams

Goodnight my precious little one,

I'll tuck you into bed.

For sweet dreams are awaiting you,

My little sleepyhead.

Grandpa's

Upstairs at Grandpa's is your favorite spot,

You find lots of treasures that you like a lot.

For Mommy grew up there and left behind

Dolls, games and books of all kinds.

"When we straightaway get there, I'm going upstairs,"

Is a phrase that I often hear you declare.

For there's so much hunting and searching to do,

Through boxes, shelves and dresser drawers, too.

And then you ask Mom if the things that you find,

Can be brought home, and she doesn't mind.

For the one she's been saving these special things for

Is the one with his arms full, waiting at the door.

Stew-a-blini Soup

Your stew-a-blini soup that you made us at the park,

Tasted quite delicious, but it was getting dark.

So we packed up your pans

and measuring cups and spoons,

And told you we'd go back there very, very soon.

We asked you what was in your stew

and you just scratched your head,

You thought about it for a while,

then this is what you said . . .

Tons of salt, tons of pepper,

tons of ice cream, mushrooms, too.

Next you added flour and water to your delicious stew.

You say you want to be a cook just like your daddy is.

If you keep cooking things like this

you'll surely be a whiz.

Morgan

Morgan's our cat who's gray, striped and fat.

He has a long tail that goes this way and that.

He prefers to stay outside on hot summer days,

But when winter comes, he changes his ways.

For then he stays inside as cozy as can be,

Next to a fire with you and me.

Or in his chair, that's just the right size,

For him to curl up in and close his eyes.

For most of the day he likes to sleep,

Quietly dreaming, not making a peep.

But when nighttime comes, he's ready to play.

Why go to bed now? he seems to say.

He likes playing with straws, scratching a box,

And covering his food up with Daddy's old socks.

He jumps on the couch and licks our hands,

He wants us to pet him, we understand.

Morgan likes our company, and we like his, too.

Oh, without Morgan . . .

What would we do?

James

James lives by Grandpa—right next door.

He is three and you are four.

When you're together, you have so much fun,

You like building worm castles out in the sun.

And then you ask Grandpa to please get your bike

Because James is riding his little trike.

You draw beautiful pictures with sidewalk chalk,

And then go with Grandpa and me on our walks.

And when James is napping, you hardly can wait.

For him to wake up before it's too late.

There's just so much playing, so much to do,

Before Daddy picks up Mommy and you.

But don't you worry,

We'll be back.

Before you know it, my little Zach.

My Prayer

I beg to be healed and strengthened each day,

For I know that you need me and want me to stay.

Butterflies

Kathy found two caterpillars out on her deck,

They were eating her parsley—she was a wreck.

So she put 'em in a jar and left it at our door,

We gave them some sticks, parsley and more.

They grew nice and fat and soon, very soon,

We hoped they'd start building their little cocoons.

When they decided that the time was just right,

They started their cocoons one hot summer night.

By morning they were finished—that part was done,

So we put 'em on a shelf out of the sun.

We patiently waited, then waited some more,

And then came the day we were hoping for.

Right there before our eyes,

Was a beautiful swallowtail butterfly.

We opened the jar, and he spread his wings

And was off to discover many new things.

And then in just about a day,

The other one came out to play.

We'll never forget that beautiful sight,

Of those swallowtail butterflies in flight.

Ovarian Cancer—Summary/Lessons Learned

It was during my ovarian cancer that I experienced the most difficult time of my life. Bald, weaker than weak, dropping weight quickly and suffering daily side effects from the chemotherapy, I was in the deepest, darkest pit of my life. At thirty-three years old, my whole world had come crashing down.

While undergoing intensive chemotherapy for the cancer, I felt as if I were literally hanging onto life by a thin thread—immensely struggling just to make it through each day. Fear reigned in my heart as I came face to face with my own immortality. This, in hindsight, was actually a blessing. For when I was face to face with death, I cried out to God. I began to seek Him through prayer and Bible reading. Daily, I cried out to Him for courage, hope, peace, love, faith, healing and joy. And as I sought God, He began to reveal Himself to me, through the Bible, prayer, other believers and my circumstances.

In January of 1992, I asked Jesus into my heart to be my personal Savior and Lord of my life. That day, I truly came to life, a new life, a life full of meaning and purpose—an abundant life in Jesus.

With Jesus in my heart, I still had to undergo more difficult chemotherapy treatments, I still had to daily face the reality of my disease, and I still had to endure countless doctor visits, blood tests, MRIs, CT scans, daily shots to raise my white blood cell counts, hospital stays, and more. But Jesus gave me strength for each day and hope for the next. He reminded me that I wasn't home yet and that the best was yet to come. He also brought a peace and a joy that I had never known before. An incredible peace and joy that remained with me regardless of my circumstances.

I learned so much during my ovarian cancer. Looking back, twelve specific lessons come to mind.

1. I learned the truth that God loves me more than I can even imagine, that He loves me unconditionally, a kind of love I hadn't experienced before. A kind of love that isn't dependent on anything I do or say. Relief flooded my heart as I realized that I could never *earn* God's love but only needed to *accept* it.

2. I learned the truth about Jesus—that He *paid in full* the penalty for my sins, my raggedness, and that my salvation depended on what He had done, not on my good deeds, church attendance or anything else. I learned that I needed to accept what Jesus had done for me at the cross by asking Him into my heart to be my Savior and Lord of my life in order to have peace with God and eternal life. I learned that Jesus is the One who never changes, the One I can always depend on, the One who sets us free.

3. I learned the truth that the Bible is my map for life and that God speaks to me personally through it. I began reading the Bible with a teachable heart, hungry to hear from Him. And as I began reading the Bible, I began hearing God for the first time ever. God used the Bible to comfort me, encourage me, strengthen me, guide me and more. It was during my ovarian cancer that the Bible became an integral

part of my everyday life. Psalm 119:92 perfectly sums up my feelings back then, "If your law had not been my delight, I would have perished in my affliction" (NIV).

4. I learned to pray. I mean pray! Cancer has a way of turning even the most calloused people into prayer warriors! It was during that cancer that prayer became an important part of my everyday life. I learned to pray about everything—not just crisis situations. I learned to cast my cares on God through prayer (at times over and over again!) and I learned how to go before God's throne— humbly, boldly, persistently and with specific prayer requests. I also learned that since prayer is communication with God, it should include listening. I had never before in my life listened to God in prayer. That was a major discovery on my journey.

5. I learned to praise God. As you recall, Don told me to praise God one day. Initially, I thought he was crazy. I was so weak I could barely crawl to the bathroom, and he was telling me to praise God? After reading an article on praise from Don, I tried praising God, even though at the time I didn't really feel like it. Afterwards, something indescribable happened deep inside my soul, and I have continued praising God in good times and in bad.

6. I learned to walk by faith, not by sight. During my cancer, I dropped from around 130 pounds down to 90 pounds. My knees were bigger than my legs. I was skin and bones. Through reading the Bible, God gave me specific verses to personally claim for my situation at the time, verses that

spoke of healing and of life on this earth. I chose to believe God's words to me then and to walk by faith, even when the doctors were negative—even when "by sight" I looked like I was on the brink of death.

7. Face to face with death, I learned that life truly is a gift. I no longer took life for granted like I had for so many years when I was healthy. Instead, I learned to thank God each and every morning for life . . . for another day . . . .a gift from His hand. A joy bubbled up inside me as I pictured unwrapping the gift of each new day.

8. I learned that *I* have control over my attitude. After hearing that fact and thinking about it, I realized that, daily, I had been letting my circumstances determine my attitude. Relief flooded my heart as I realized I didn't have to live another day in that prison of crummy attitudes. From that day forward, with God's help, I determined to greet each day with a positive attitude instead of the negative one I had been lugging around. And, amazingly, as I became more positive, those around me did, too. Attitudes can be contagious!

9. I learned and experienced the truth that nothing is impossible with God. God planted that seed of truth in my life early on during my cancer. And after watching the miracle of healing that He performed in my life, both physically and spiritually, that seed of truth took root and blossomed into an unwavering belief that nothing *is* impossible with God. I believe it with every ounce of my being. God has brought that truth to my mind many times throughout

my journey. He has shown me over and over that my seemingly impossible situations are merely a stage upon which He can reveal His power, His love, His mercy and more. For *nothing* is impossible with Him.

10. I learned to wait on God. God brought Isaiah 40:31 to my mind over and over during that time: "But they that wait upon the Lord shall renew their strength. They shall mount up with wings like eagles; they shall run and not be weary; they shall walk and not faint." I prayed and I prayed, and then I waited and waited for some of those answers to arrive. Learning to wait on God is not an easy lesson to learn, especially living in the fast-driven society in which I do. But through waiting on God, precious jewels were formed in my life; jewels of patience, strength, and a deeper knowledge of Him. Waiting on God is worth the wait . . . every single time.

11. I learned how to deal with fear. Fear is a very real thing and a lousy traveling companion. It is always trying to steal our joy. During my cancer, there were days I was paralyzed by fear. But then one day, I came across a verse in Isaiah that said, "He will keep in perfect peace those whose thoughts turn often to the Lord." *Perfect peace . . .* in the midst of cancer? Wow. That's what I wanted. God clearly spoke to me through that verse in Isaiah. With His help, I took my thoughts captive (2 Corinthians 10:5, NRSV) and kept my thoughts on Him when I came face to face with fear. And once I started doing my part (i.e. keeping my thoughts on the Lord), the Lord took care of

the rest and supplied His perfect peace—even in the midst of cancer. I discovered that keeping my thoughts on the Lord was a powerful weapon in battling my fears.

I also discovered that God's Word, the Bible, is another powerful weapon in battling fear. In Ephesians 6:17, we're told that God's Word is "the sword of the Spirit." Once I learned that truth, I began to memorize various Bible verses such as Philippians 4:13 "I can do all things through Him who strengthens me" (NRSV); Philippians 4:6 "Don't worry about anything, instead pray about everything"; and Psalm 105:4 "Seek the Lord and His strength; seek His presence continually" (NRSV). Back then, when I felt fear seizing my heart, I would repeat one of those memorized verses over and over in my mind, or out loud, until my fears were relieved. Sometimes, though, no sooner had my fears gone than they returned. So, again, I would repeat the verses until my fears were again relieved.

Prayer is another powerful weapon for battling fear. And there were times back then when all I said in prayer was, "Help!" At those times God knew my desperation and somehow sent the help I needed. Sometimes the help came in the form of a friend's encouraging words, a song I heard, or in a card. Although the gift and wrapping varied, one thing was certain—help always arrived when I needed it most. While writing these thoughts about dealing with fear, I came across the following poem in a devotional, which perfectly describes my feelings during my ovarian cancer. "A tempest great of doubt and fear possessed my mind; no light was there to guide, or make my vision clear. Dark night! 'Twas more than I could bear then He arose I saw His face—there was a calm filled with His grace." Streams in the Dessert

I, also, came across a poem that I had written a few years later during cancer #2. It also relates to fear, along with God's Word, "the sword of the Spirit."

Last night, when all was quiet
there were tears upon my bed.
The pain so unrelenting,
Raging battle in my head.
On one side was the enemy,
saying God won't see you through;
But the Spirit, which was stronger,
said God's promises are true.

My sword was right beside me, and I drew it right away.
I got into the Psalms and let it open where it may.
God's Spirit took me by the hand to help me clear my mind,
And once again the enemy was defeated, left behind.

Finally, another way I learned to battle fear was to remember truths about God, that He is in control, He is faithful, He is loving. Remembering those truths made God appear even bigger in my mind, which always made my problems appear smaller.

At times, fear still harasses me, and occasionally I'm even caught in it's grip—but not for long. Invariably, God stirs my memory and reminds me of the lessons He taught me during my ovarian cancer—the actions I need to take to experience

His peace. Thankfully, I am no longer a slave to fear like I once was. "Thanks be to God who gives us the victory through our Lord Jesus Christ."

12. I learned that no matter what my situation is, there is always someone who is worse off than I am. One day while I waited to undergo a procedure at the hospital, I was feeling extremely sorry for myself. I was literally skin and bones, and my white count was under 1.0. I was so very sick. As I waited for my name to be called, a patient was wheeled past me in a wheelchair. It was the first person I had seen who actually looked sicker than I did. Drowning in hospital attire, sunk down in the wheelchair and wearing a facemask to protect him from germs, he looked like he was on the brink of death. I was shocked at his appearance, and at that moment, Pete said to me, "No matter what your situation is, there is always someone who is worse off than you are." Upon hearing those words, my perspective was immediately changed. I have never forgotten Pete's words to me, or the image of that gravely sick individual. They continue to impact my perspective daily. Perspective is an important element on the cancer journey.

I am forever grateful that God healed me physically and spiritually. I'm also grateful for the life-changing truths and messages God taught me. They are threads of gold now tightly woven into the tapestry of my life by the Master Weaver, my Heavenly Father—the One who knew just when and where to place those threads of gold.

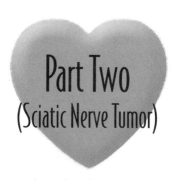

Part Two
(Sciatic Nerve Tumor)

Angel in Disguise

Listen to my pleading, Lord! Be merciful and send the help I need. (Psalm 27:7)

After months of going from doctor to doctor, there I was in a chiropractor's office. An earlier scan had revealed a couple of slight degenerative discs, and major leg and back pain marked my days. I had already tried physical therapy, but it hadn't relieved my pain. After praying for God's wisdom for the doctors, and guidance for me, a relative suggested I make an appointment with his chiropractor. Well, I did that and there I was sitting in the waiting room . . . hopeful for some relief.

After being treated by the chiropractor that day, I still didn't feel any relief. I told myself, though, that it was just too early to tell if the scheduled treatments would help or not. So before leaving the chiropractor's office I made another appointment. After that next appointment I made another appointment, then another, then another . . . still struggling with pain.

One day, my pain was almost unbearable as I sat in the chiropractor's room waiting for my name to be called. While waiting, my eyes spotted a brochure on a wire rack across from where I was sitting. The title of the brochure was "Pain—An Angel in Disguise." Pain an angel? Yeah, right, I thought to myself, moments before my name was called and I was taken to a treatment room.

For some reason, though, my mind kept returning to the title of that brochure during the days that followed my visit. "Pain, An Angel in Disguise." Amazingly, the more it came to mind, the more I found myself agreeing with it. Angels are messengers, I thought to myself. My pain *is* sending messages to my brain that something is wrong with my body. From that day forward, I looked at my pain in a whole new light, and I continued to pray for wisdom for the doctors and guidance for myself.

After several appointments with the chiropractor, I was disappointed to hear him say that the chiropractic treatments should have brought relief by now (which they hadn't). He then graciously referred me to a doctor at the University of Minnesota who he thought might be able to help me. The University doctor was an orthopedic surgeon who was apparently highly regarded in his field.

As soon as I got home from my chiropractor's office that day, I made the call to the University and set up an appointment with the recommended specialist. *Please Lord, give him wisdom*, I silently prayed.

The day arrived for my appointment at the University, and Pete accompanied me there. After meeting my new doctor, I relayed my symptoms to him. After listening to me and examining me he looked puzzled. Orthopedically, he told me, things were looking okay. "Are you sure they checked for possible recurrent ovarian cancer?" he asked. I assured him that a few months earlier I had undergone an MRI and another scan that had only revealed a couple of degenerative discs. I left his office that day with instructions to see my oncologist again. I called the following day to set up an appointment with her.

At my appointment I began to tell the oncologist my saga of the past month and why I had ended up back at her office. I then gingerly got up onto the examining table and she examined me. I told her about my appointment with the University doctor who thought I may have cancer again. "You do not have cancer!" she curtly replied. "Well," I said, "he suggested that I have another MRI because of my symptoms."

At that point my oncologist got on the phone to talk to the University doctor herself. After talking with him she decided to order another MRI just to be safe. At the same time, she prescribed some pain medication for me, too. My pain, however, still felt like a knife and sliced through even the new pain medication.

A few days later, I called to talk to my oncologist. I needed a stronger pain medication, and I also wanted to find out about my MRI results. On the phone with her office, the receptionist acted strangely evasive and finally said that my doctor would have to call me back. I hung up the phone and wondered why the receptionist had acted so strangely. Had they seen something on my MRI?

Shortly after my conversation with my oncologist's receptionist, I got a call from my oncologist herself. "My pain is unbelievable," I told her immediately. "I need a stronger pain medication." I could hardly believe what I heard next. "You need to check yourself into the hospital. They found something on your scan that needs to be biopsied." I don't recall anything else she said. I hung up the phone and cried. Pain truly was an angel in disguise.

Angels Around Me

For He will command His angels concerning you . . . (Psalm 91:11, NRSV)

My oncologist's words played over and over in my mind like a scratched CD.

Unfortunately, Pete was out of town on business that day. After pulling myself together, I called his boss, Tony. I quickly explained my circumstances to Tony and the fact that I really needed Pete home—as soon as possible. Tony said that he'd try to locate Pete, and he also tried to encourage me by reminding me that we didn't know yet whether I had cancer or not. I hung up the phone, and shortly thereafter Pete called. Sadness and shock traveled the phone line before Pete told me that he'd catch the soonest possible flight home.

Between prayers and tears I called my dad and my dear sister in Christ, Deb. They were shocked by my news, even though they had been aware of the pain I had been struggling with for months.

Dad was the first to arrive at our place after I had spoken to him and Deb. The sadness he was feeling inside was written all over his face. He came inside and hugged me. We then sat on our porch together . . . silently sharing the sadness.

After a little while, I called my pastor to tell him the circumstances and to see if he could possibly come to our house. He said that he could. Shortly after my conversation with him, Deb was at our door, full of hugs and tears. Deb joined Dad and me on the porch and offered a prayer. As the three of us prayed, I felt strengthened . . . reminded of God's faithfulness. Afterwards, I reminded myself that God would surely see me through.

Our pastor was the next to arrive, and he joined our brokenhearted little group. He read some Scripture to us and then prayed. An air of sadness filled the porch that day that is hard to describe. Waves of complete silence rolled in upon us.

During one of those waves of silence, I was reminded of a song that God had inspired me to write just days prior. It had come to me the day of the scheduled MRI. I decided then to sing it for the group gathered on our porch . . .

The Lord is my strength,
My rock, and my salvation.
I won't be afraid.
I will call on Him.

He is there for the good times
And holds us through the bad,
Just the kind of friend
That we always wished we had.

He will always be right near us,
Showing us the way,
Lighting up our path
To never ending day.

And I found it to be true
That when I'm weak I'm strong.
God fills me with His strength
And helps me to go on.

After singing it, I felt His strength upholding me. And with my Heavenly focus restored, peace and joy returned to my heart.

Through that song, I was reminded that God *was* near and listening to our heart's cry—that He *was* my strength, my rock and my salvation and always would be, no matter what. Though I was weak, He was strong.

After our pastor left to do the rest of God's appointed work for him that day, a truck pulled up into our driveway. Unsure of who it was, I waited, watched and soon realized it was a friend of mine and her husband. How had they heard about my situation? I wondered. Well, it turned out they hadn't. They were just in the neighborhood and were stopping by to check out our living room floor for ideas to use in their own house. For months, that friend had been telling me she wanted to stop and see our newly redone living room floor. Only she had never gotten around to stopping by until then.

Isn't God amazing? He always sends His angels just when we need them. Never early, never late . . . on time . . . His time. The angels come in love, always exuding the fragrance of His presence. Psalm 91:11 says, "For He will command His angels concerning you" (NRSV). By the time my friend and her husband left, I felt wrapped in God's amazing love.

A short time later, Pete arrived home from his shortened business trip. When I saw him walking up our sidewalk, I sensed another of God's angels had arrived. He hugged me, kissed me and told me I'd be okay. We then quickly packed a bag for me, made arrangements for Zach, and then made our way to the hospital.

On the way to the hospital, I considered God's workings in my life that day, and I was reminded of the fact that He was in control. He had helped Tony quickly locate Pete who was out of town, He had helped Pete arrive home quickly without a hitch, He had arranged for Dad, Deb and our pastor to be with me in Pete's absence, He had reminded me of that inspired song just when I needed to remember it's message and He had arranged the unexpected visit by friends just when I was in need of support. Yes, He was in control and like that inspired song said, "God fills me with His strength and helps me to go on." I knew then that He would help me to go on . . .

Heavenly Strength

When you lie down, you will not be afraid; Yes, you will lie down and your sleep will be sweet. (Proverbs 3:24, NKJV)

With the news from the doctor fresh on our minds—the news that they had seen something on my MRI—Pete and I drove to the hospital in silence . . . in shock. At the hospital, I was assigned a room, and a nurse helped me to get settled in.

After that, an array of hospital staff came to talk to me. Among those were my gynecologist and the IV team, who thankfully hooked me up to an IV for pain medication.

Once the pain medication began to work, my brain was freed up to think about other things. Other things besides pain, that is. By that time, Pete had gone home, and I soon found myself being smothered by unsettling thoughts. Thoughts that included my gynecologist's words to me that night.

My gynecologist told me that I had a mass wrapped around my sciatic nerve. Ouch! No wonder I was in pain! He also told me that he was going to perform a needle biopsy on it the next morning and went on to explain that since the mass was located near a large artery there was some risk involved in performing the biopsy. He also said that my oncologist thought the mass was cancerous. He, on the other hand, wasn't convinced. His words raced round and round in my mind, and like I mentioned, I felt smothered by them. Fear was quickly gaining ground in my mind. I was exhausted, too. I hadn't slept at all the night before because of the pain, and I knew I desperately needed to get some sleep. Before I went to sleep, I tried to pray, but I just couldn't concentrate. What if the needle slipped during the biopsy and hit that large artery? What if I had cancer again? What if? What if? What if?

It was then I felt the Holy Spirit nudging me to read my Bible, which was next to me on the hospital tray. I reached for it, but before opening it, I prayed for God to give me scripture that would meet me where I was at—scripture that would restore my peace.

After that short prayer to God, I opened my Bible and my eyes landed on Isaiah 41:10, "Do not fear, for I am with you, do not be afraid, for I am your God; I will strengthen you, I will help you, I will uphold you with my victorious right hand" (NRSV). I sensed God clearly speaking to me. I read Isaiah 41:10 again and again. Marveling at my Heavenly Father . . . marveling at His tender words of comfort to me. I knew then I had nothing to fear. I was reminded that God was with me. And whether the mass was cancerous or not, He would uphold me with His victorious right hand.

At that moment God's heaven-sent peace, which is hard to fully describe, yet so very real, filled my heart, and my fears vanished. I closed my Bible and then my eyes. I fell fast asleep wrapped in God's peace. As I write these words, Psalm 127: 2 comes to mind, "For he gives sleep to His beloved" (NRSV). And I think to myself—even the night before a needle biopsy that may hit an artery or that may uncover cancer—He gives sleep to His beloved . . .

When I awoke the next morning, God's peace remained. So did Isaiah 41:10. Shortly after the needle biopsy I found out that the mass on my sciatic nerve was indeed cancerous. After hearing the news that I had cancer once again, I remembered Isaiah 41:10. And when I did, by God's grace, I chose to believe God—to take Him at His word. He was my God, the One who would strengthen me and help me, the One who would indeed uphold me with His victorious right hand.

P.S. When I received a card from our church the next week, I smiled as I read the imprinted verse on it—Isaiah 41:10.

Relief on the Horizon

The same day I found out the results of my needle biopsy (that I did indeed have cancer again), I was scheduled to meet with a radiation doctor.

My meeting with the radiation doctor was brief. After looking at my MRI and other vital information earlier, he had determined that radiation was definitely what I needed first—followed up by chemotherapy. He told me that the tumor had to be shrunk as quickly as possible to relieve the debilitating pain I was experiencing. And in his opinion, he believed that radiation treatments would accomplish that goal the most effectively.

I left that appointment filled with hope. The pain that had marked my days and crowded my thoughts was going to be attacked head on . . . in just a few days from then. Relief was on the horizon. God would uphold me with His victorious right hand . . .

A Dilemma and a Prayer

Trust in the Lord with all your heart, and do not rely on your own insight. In all your ways acknowledge Him, and He will make straight your paths. (Proverbs 3:5–6, NRSV)

After my appointment with the radiation doctor and before my appointment with my oncologist, I halfheartedly asked Pete, "What if my two doctors don't agree on the best treatment program for me?" "We'll just have to wait and see," Pete answered. I sensed then that that thought had never crossed his mind. And I wondered then why in the world it was on my mine . . .

A few days after my appointment with my radiation doctor I had an appointment with my oncologist. Pete and I arrived right on time. I had made sure we hadn't gotten there early. It was the last place I wanted to be.

When my oncologist entered the office where Pete and I were waiting for her, an air of grimness followed her in and hung around for our entire meeting.

With my chart in hand she told me that the mass on my sciatic nerve was inoperable. She told me that she was sorry. She said that I needed to start chemotherapy treatments the next day. She told me the name of the chemotherapy drug that I would be receiving and . . . whoaaa! . . . just a minute!, I thought to myself. Chemotherapy the next day?! What about radiation?

At that point in our conversation I spoke up. I told her the radiation doctor had recommended radiation first, followed by chemotherapy. She heard me out and then proceeded to discuss the two options with us. She, too, had looked at my MRI and other vital information. In her judgment, chemotherapy was the best treatment option for arresting the cancer.

Thinking that she had convinced me to start chemotherapy, she began to tell us when I should check into the hospital the next day. I think she was shocked to hear me say, "I need some time. I'm not starting chemotherapy tomorrow."

Pete and I left her office confused. I never honestly thought that my two doctors would actually disagree about my treatment plan, even though I had considered the possibility following my meeting with the radiation doctor.

On the way to the car, my mind raced that day. I thought about the fact that my oncologist had been my doctor for four years. Surely she knew my body and what would be best. But chemotherapy? The next day?

I wasn't feeling peace with her plan at all, and Pete wasn't either. In fact, I had never seen him with such a restless spirit. He seemed to be tossing about in waves of confusion.

As we drove home in silence from my oncologist's office something occurred to me. That something was the fact that even though *I* didn't have a clue about what my body needed, God did. For Psalm 139:13 says, "You made all the delicate, inner parts of my body, and knit them together in my mother's womb." I pondered that new thought the rest of the way home. When we arrived home, I told Pete my thoughts— that *God* knew exactly what my body needed and that we needed to ask Him for guidance. Right then and there, on our porch, Pete and I bowed our heads in prayer. We poured out our hearts to God and asked Him for His help, His guidance.

Proverbs 3:5–6 tells us to "Trust in the Lord with all your heart, and do not rely on your own insight. In all your ways acknowledge Him, and He will make straight your paths"(NRSV). God had guided us before and I believed with all my heart that He would guide us again. I never dreamt His answer would come so quickly . . .

A New Path

I will instruct you and teach you the way you should go . . . (Psalm 32:8, NRSV)

Within an hour of our prayer for God's help and guidance, my dear sister in Christ, Maureen and her husband Jake, were at our door with dinner. Maureen was part of my Bible study group that was bringing meals for us following my Cancer #2 diagnosis. That particular night was Maureen's scheduled turn.

We invited Maureen and Jake in, and after a bit of small talk, we got more serious. We explained to them our dilemma, the fact that my two doctors disagreed on the best treatment option for me.

Upon hearing our dilemma, Maureen and Jake began to talk. They told us that they had a friend who was an oncologist. In fact, Maureen had mentioned that friend to me before, but I had never really given it much thought. Maureen and Jake went on to tell us what a wonderfully warm and caring doctor she was. They also offered to call her and talk with her regarding my situation. In fact, they ended up calling her before they left our house that night.

After the phone call with their friend, Dr. Bowers, they told me that she had agreed to see me. I just needed to call her office the next day and set up an appointment. Was God at work already? I silently wondered.

Maureen and Jake left our house shortly after their conversation with Dr. Bowers. When they were gone, I looked at Pete and noticed that he was beaming. His restless spirit quieted, I could sense the peace that he was experiencing. Pete told me then that he felt sure that I was supposed to see Dr. Bowers. I felt better about my situation, but still not completely at peace. Sure, it was easy for Pete, Maureen and Jake to tell me to go to another doctor, but it wasn't that easy for me to even consider that option. I knew that I would go for a second opinion, but change doctors? I wasn't so sure about that.

The oncologist I had been seeing knew my medical history better than any other doctor. She had seen me through my original diagnosis, treatment, and continued follow-up. She was extremely well respected in the medical community, and although she didn't have the greatest bedside manner, I was used to it. The more I began thinking about my oncologist, the more I realized that I didn't want to change doctors ... but I wondered then if *God* was directing me to.

A short time after Maureen and Jake left our house, the phone rang. Pete answered, and I heard him telling the person on the other end of the phone our dilemma and, also, what had happened during Maureen and Jake's visit.

When Pete got off the phone and joined me in the other room, he was beaming even more. "That was Jill." (Jill was another dear sister in Christ from my Bible study group.) Pete went on to tell me how excited Jill was to hear that I was going to see Dr. Bowers. Then Pete said something that really grabbed my attention. He said, "Jill told me that some of your friends from Bible study have been praying that you would go to a different oncologist." I wondered ... was my prayer for guidance leading me to a different oncologist, the same thing my Bible study friends had been praying all along? I sensed God was at work, and like the old saying about killing two birds with one stone, maybe God was answering two different prayers with one answer.

I knew from the Bible and past experience that God always knows what's best for us at all times. By the time of my appointment with Dr. Bowers the next day, I was willing to consider changing doctors if I knew for sure it was God's will for me. I remembered an old saying about prayer changing us more than anything, and I knew then that my heart truly had been changed by prayer.

When I met Dr. Bowers, I liked her immediately. She had a warmth about her that I had rarely seen in a doctor. At one point during my appointment with her, I mentioned the name of the University doctor I had seen, Dr. Transfeldt. He was the doctor responsible for pursuing my case until the correct diagnosis was made. Upon hearing Dr. Transfeldt's name, Dr. Bowers told me that her daughter was a friend of Dr. Transfeldt's daughter. Coincidence? No. God at work? Yes. I knew it in my heart for sure.

After reviewing my case, Dr. Bowers said she believed radiation was the way to go, followed by chemotherapy. I told her then the name of the radiation doctor I had seen, Dr. Sperduto. I was amazed at her next words to me—Dr. Sperduto was her husband's partner.

I was convinced then that I needed to change doctors and that radiation was what my body needed first—followed up by chemotherapy. My feelings of uncertainty melted away right then and there and were replaced by peace. God's peace. God was leading and I would follow. Even if it were down a new path—even if it were to a new doctor.

I remembered again the truth that God knows what is best for me at all times. And I considered the fact anew that He created me and knows me inside and out. And like Jeremiah 29:11 tells me, His plans for me are for good not evil. Yes, God was leading and I would follow . . .

Radiation and the Nurse

My grace* is sufficient for you, for my power is made perfect in weakness. (2 Corinthians 12:9, NIV)

*Grace—the undeserved kindness and mercy that God gives us.

The day is forever etched on my mind, and I will never forget it. The day, that is, that I met with my radiation doctor just prior to beginning radiation treatments for the malignant tumor wrapped around my sciatic nerve. During that appointment with my new radiation doctor, I had measurements taken for my radiation treatments, and I also got a radiation "tattoo" applied.

I can still picture myself earlier in our bathroom getting ready for that appointment with my radiation doctor—putting on my makeup and fixing my hair. I also remember the questions that raced in my mind while I got ready that morning. What will radiation be like? How will it affect me physically? When will the pain go away?

With those questions on my mind, a song came to me. An inspired song, fresh from God: "*I'm counting on grace, Lord, to see me through. I'm counting on grace, Lord, that comes from you.*" With that little song on my mind, I realized that God's grace was indeed what I needed to see me through my scheduled radiation treatments. I prayed for God's grace right then and there.

I took my time getting ready for the appointment that day. In fact, I dragged my feet, apprehensive about what radiation therapy would be like. Eventually, though, it was time to go.

The song that God had inspired me with continued to play on my mind all the way to the hospital. It strengthened me and kept my focus heavenly—on the Lord. When Pete and I arrived at the hospital, we checked in at the radiation department and were told to have a seat in the waiting area.

After a short wait, a nurse called my name and brought Pete and me to a room where we would meet with the doctor. While we waited, I stretched out on the examining table. I had discovered that lying down somewhat eased the excruciating pain from the tumor.

While on the examining table, there was a knock on the door. Then a nurse entered and closed the door behind her. Looking at her, I realized it was a different nurse than the one who had escorted us to the room. "Hi, my name is *Grace*," she said. "I'll be your radiation nurse." At that moment, the words of that little song God had inspired me with earlier came back to me. "*I'm counting on grace, Lord, to see me through. I'm counting on grace, Lord, that comes from you.*" At that moment I sensed God at work, and my heart began dancing with joy.

I saw Grace every day of my radiation treatments and when I did, I sensed God's presence, that His grace surely would see me through. Which it did. Just like 2 Corinthians 12:9 says, "My grace is sufficient for you, for my power is made perfect in weakness" (NIV).

During those days of radiation, I realized anew that each day was a gift, wrapped in God's grace. And although the "grace-wrapping" changes, depending on our circumstances, one thing is certain. No matter what God calls us to do or to be, His grace is sufficient. It will always see us through . . . *He will always see us through.*

P.S.S. See Part Four: *For my Good*

My Sovereign Lord

How great you are, O Sovereign Lord! There is no one like you, and there is no God but you . . .
(2 Samuel 7:22, NIV)

After getting my radiation "tattoo" applied, I was ready to begin radiation treatments. Even though the next weekend was July fourth, a holiday weekend, Dr. Sperduto scheduled me for a Saturday appointment. His goal through radiation was to shrink the inoperable, malignant tumor as soon as possible, in order to relieve my pain.

When I arrived at the radiation department that Saturday, I was met by Dr. Sperduto and a female technician. The two of them walked me to the room where I would receive my radiation treatments. While the technician got me situated, Dr. Sperduto left the room.

At that time, when radiation treatments were given, custom blocks were made to guide the radiation to the exact location in the body. My custom blocks weren't done yet, so the technician had to manually set up hand blocks.

On the table, while I waited for the technician to finish preparations, I fervently prayed. I specifically asked God to guide the technician as she worked on the radiation setup details for my body. The stakes were high, and I didn't want her to mess up!

When the technician was done getting everything ready, Dr. Sperduto appeared again. He asked the technician how it was going as he walked over to where she was working. He then checked out the setup for himself. As I listened, I heard Dr. Sperduto change something. And then he told the technician, "It should be like that instead."

Lying on that radiation table that day, thanks and praise filled my heart. God was indeed near and listening to my prayer. Though unrecognizable to the technician and Dr. Sperduto, my Sovereign Heavenly Father was directing them from above.

Daniel 4:35 says, "He does as He pleases with the powers of heaven and the peoples of the earth. No one can hold back His hand or say to Him: "What have you done?" (NIV) According to Psalm 135:6, "The Lord does whatever pleases Him, in the heavens and on the earth, in the seas and all their depths" (NIV).

No matter what chapter of my life God is writing, I am always comforted when I remember the fact that *He* is in control. For He is love and He is faithful. And I can't think of anyone better to be in control. Of all things in heaven—and on earth.

P.S. After I wrote the ending to this story, I took a shower. While in the shower, God inspired me with this little saying, "God is in control, God is in control. And knowing that brings comfort to a tired and weary soul." Yes! God *is* in control. Spread the word. Pass it on . . .

God's Message Loud and Clear

Man looks at the outward appearance, but the Lord looks at the heart. (1 Samuel 16:7, NIV)

One morning while undergoing chemotherapy for my sciatic nerve tumor, I had a conversation with God about my bald head. It was the second time I had lost my hair due to chemotherapy. I told God that particular morning how crazy I thought I looked bald and how unbecoming it was for a woman.

After discussing my baldness with God for several minutes He impressed 1 Samuel 16:7 on my heart, which says, "Man looks at the outward appearance but the Lord looks at the heart" (NIV). After receiving God's reply, I went to make breakfast and felt a little foolish that I had even brought up the bald subject!

As I made myself breakfast that morning, I was listening to my favorite Christian radio station. You can imagine my surprise when the radio pastor said, "Man looks at the outward appearance, God looks at the heart." God's message to me was loud and clear that day. Bald head or not, my heart is what is important to Him—a fact that I sometimes forget living in the world I do, a world obsessed with physical appearances.

I never brought up the bald subject again with God. His perspective regarding my bald head became my perspective. It was then I drew a smiley face on a sweatshirt with these words written underneath it: "*Praise God Even on a Bad Hair Day.*"

Lemon Drops

What do you have there in your hand?" the Lord asked him. And he replied, "A shepherd's rod." "Throw it down on the ground," the Lord told him. So he threw it down—and it became a serpent, and Moses ran from it! (Exodus 4:2–4)

It was a Saturday morning . . . a beautiful summer day full of sunshine. My family was off running errands, and I was sitting on our porch alone feeling sorry for myself. I was in the midst of radiation treatments, and the reality of my sciatic nerve tumor had hit home. Tears began running down my face. I cried hard for several minutes. Then, through my tears, I saw someone pulling into our driveway. When that someone got out of her van, I recognized that it was my dear sister-in-Christ, Jill, whom I had met through Bible study at our church.

When Jill saw me and my tear-stained face, she joined me on the porch to listen and to encourage me for a while. Eventually, I found out her reason for stopping by that Saturday morning—to drop off some lemon drops. I sat stunned when she handed me the package. I asked Jill then if

I had ever told her that lemon drops were my absolute favorite candy. "No," came her quick reply.

Through a little bag of lemon drops, I sensed the reality of God's presence and love for me in the midst of my pain and sorrow. I was strengthened, comforted, and my sorrow turned to joy.

The Bible abounds with stories of how God uses little things to accomplish His purposes. Little things like a rod, a sling and a stone, some bread and fish, a lowly manger, a handful of flour and a little cooking oil. Lemon drops, to this day, remind me that God is still in the business of using little things to accomplish His purposes, which is good news for me—and for you. For in this world, little things still abound. Like a cup of cold water, a smile, a phone call, a card, an encouraging word. The saying goes, "It's the little things that count." With those lemon drops on my mind, my version says, "It's the little things in God's hands that truly count" . . . this side of heaven and beyond.

A Bumper Sticker and a Sign

You will keep him in perfect peace, whose mind is stayed on you, because he trusts in you. (Isaiah 26:3, NKJV)

Set your mind on things above, not on earthly things. (Colossians 3:2, NKJV)

Many memories come to mind when I think of past Florida vacations, but one in particular always stands out for me. I vividly remember the day when our son Zach, my brother, my sister-in-law and I went to the Babcock Farms, a tourist attraction in Florida.

The four of us woke up early the morning of our scheduled trip. We ate breakfast, showered, grabbed the cameras and were off. When we arrived at Babcock Farms, we bought our tickets and soon boarded a dune buggy-type bus to make our way through a swamp. Zach was having a blast being in a swamp and looking at all the animals. I was, too, until the end of the tour, that is.

At the end of the tour, the tour guide walked down the aisle of the bus with a baby alligator. She stopped at every row of seats to let people take a look at it and touch it if they wanted to. When she stopped at the row in front of us I really noticed for the first time who was sitting there. It was an adorable young couple with a baby, and I assumed, the grandparents. I detected New York accents. The younger man was a handsome muscular guy and his wife, a bubbly beautiful woman. The baby was adorable and had what seemed like loving grandparents. What a picture of happiness, health and love. At least from the outside, I thought to myself.

While studying that adorable family, it was as if a boulder came crashing down on me and I remembered. I remembered the horrible back and leg pain I was experiencing. I remembered the MRI my oncologist had ordered for me when I returned to Minnesota. I remembered my cancer experience. I was filled with sadness as I looked at that family ahead of me. That sadness hung over me like a cloud as we got off the bus and headed home.

On the way home, my brother Randy said that he wanted to get a cone at Tastee Treat. The rest of us decided that we wanted a treat, too. When we got to Tastee Treat, Randy and Zach walked ahead. On the way to the Tastee Treat window, I noticed a car's bumper sticker. It said, "*Pray hard.*" That was exactly what I had needed to do. I pointed the bumper sticker out to my sister-in-law and smiled.

Standing at the Tastee Treat window I read the menu that was inside the cone-shaped building. For some reason, I read the *entire* menu. When I got to the bottom line, I could hardly believe what I read, "Don't worry—God is still in control." On a menu at Tastee Treat? I read it again just to make sure, "Don't worry—God is still in control." There it was . . . exactly what I needed to read, exactly when I needed to read it. I left Tastee Treat that day praising God. Not because the pain was gone or because I wouldn't need to go through more testing when I returned home, but because my God was still in control. All I needed to do was trust.

Looking back on that day at Babcock Farms, I'm reminded of a story in the New Testament. In Matthew 14: 25–31 we read:

> *About four o'clock in the morning Jesus came to them, walking on the water! They screamed in terror, for they thought He was a ghost. But Jesus immediately spoke to them, reassuring them. "Don't be afraid!" He said. Then Peter called to Him: "Sir, if it is really you, tell me to come over to you, walking on the water." "All right," the Lord said, "come along!" So Peter went over the side of the boat and walked on the water toward Jesus. But when he looked*

around at the high waves, he was terrified and began to sink.
"Save me, Lord!" he shouted.

In the above story, Peter stepped out of the boat in faith, and as long as he kept his eyes on Jesus, he walked on water. It was when Peter took his eyes off Jesus and looked at the high waves surrounding him that he got scared and began sinking.

That day at Babcock Farms, I, too, had taken my eyes off Jesus for a while and I, like Peter, began sinking. Thankfully, God helped to restore my Heavenly focus. Through a bumper sticker and a sign at Tastee Treat, He saved me from drowning in my own waves of despair.

One of my favorite verses, Psalm 105:4 says, "Seek the Lord and His strength; seek His presence continually" (NRSV). I have found that when I do what Psalm 105:4 tells me to do, I'm saved from sinking . . . from drowning. Psalm 105:4 is one of my spiritual life jackets—for both calm *and* troubled waters . . .

The Window Box

He who began a good work in you will carry it
on to completion until the day of Christ Jesus.
(Philippians 1:6, NIV)

The first summer we lived in our present home, I longed for a window box underneath our dining room window. I envisioned a box that overflowed with brightly colored flowers. So one day I shared my desire with Pete, and he agreed to build one with the help of our good friend, Mark. A short time later,

Pete and Mark began building it. When it was finished, they painstakingly attached it to the brick wall outside our dining room window. With the window box hung, I made a trip to our local nursery, anxious to get plants for it.

At the nursery, I was drawn to one flower in particular. It was called nasturtium. Being a novice gardener, I had never even heard of nasturtium, but it was beautiful and I decided to try my hand with it. So I bought several nasturtium plants, brought them home and got busy planting.

Soon, beautiful bright orange nasturtium flowed from the window box. When I spotted our window box I could hardly believe it was *our* window box and not our neighbors, whose gardens daily beckon neighborhood walkers to stop, look and enjoy. Unfortunately the nasturtium's beauty didn't last long, though. Aphids discovered them after only a few weeks and feasted day and night. Eventually, we were left with straggling vines and a few peach-colored blossoms. Not exactly what I had originally had in mind. Not easily defeated, though, I told myself that I'd try again next year.

When the next summer arrived, though, I found myself in the midst of radiation treatments for my sciatic nerve tumor. I didn't plant nasturtiums or anything else that summer. And every time we drove up or down our driveway, that six-foot long empty window box stared back at us. Until, that is, Marge and Karen, our dear neighbors with the beautiful gardens, graciously offered to plant it for us. It was such a loving offer, and after I accepted it, Karen got to work. I will never forget the window box that summer. It overflowed with a variety of flowers . . . brightly colored ones, pastel colored ones, tall ones, short ones, and all healthy ones. It was simply beautiful. I was truly blessed by it while undergoing my radiation treatments.

Not only was I blessed by the beauty of the flowers that summer but also by what God revealed to me through those flowers and window box. First, he showed me how my life had at one time resembled that empty six foot-long window box. The one that for weeks had stared back at us when we drove up or down our driveway. Empty pursuits and selfish desires had once marked my days. Nothing I did or received had satisfied me completely. I was empty, with no real meaning or purpose to my life. But then everything changed when I asked Jesus into my heart, to be my personal Savior and to take control of my life. After receiving Him, I felt like a new creation, and I was. For as 2 Corinthians 5:17 says, "Therefore, if anyone is in Christ, he is a new creation; the old has gone, the new has come!" (NIV) Just as the soil and flowers eventually filled up our window box, I was filled up, too (after receiving Jesus)—with God's love, peace and joy. For the first time ever, I felt satisfied and had real meaning and purpose in my life. With God's insight in hand, I realized anew that day how far I had come on the wings of grace alone, and thanks overflowed my heart.

Secondly, God showed me that like our flowers, I need spiritual light, water, and protection from my enemy: light from His Son (Jesus Christ), water from His Word (the Bible) and protection from my enemy (Satan). When a flower's needs are met, the result is beautiful. So it is when my spiritual needs are met. For when those needs are met, I am filled with His strength, His peace, His love, His joy and more. And it is then that I reflect Jesus to the lost and lonely world around me, which is indeed a beautiful sight. With that second insight from God, I was reminded of the importance of having my own spiritual needs met so that I can reflect Jesus to others and become the beautiful child of God I was created to be.

Lastly, God showed me that my life was a lot like one variety of the window box flowers, the one we waited so patiently for to bloom. We knew that one day we would wake up to beautiful blossoms—a beautiful harvest. God knows that because I am a Christian that one day I will be like Jesus. He knows that it will take grace and time, but that the wait will be worth it—the blossoms, the harvest, will be beautiful. He can already see it. With that last insight from God, I was encouraged. I remembered that becoming like Jesus is a process and that it doesn't happen overnight. When I abide in Him, I am transformed by His grace daily, and one day I *will* wake up to a beautiful harvest . . . I will be like Jesus.

I am so thankful for the insights God gave me that summer of my sciatic nerve tumor, using our window box and flowers. Those insights still remind me of all that He has done and is doing for me. Considering all of this, my heart overflows with praise. Just like our window box overflowed with flowers. And I have come to know that a heart full of praise is fertile soil in my Heavenly Father's hand. Fertile soil where He can plant His seeds of joy, peace, love and more and make them grow. The Bible says that God is the one who makes things grow. Praise be to God, the Master Gardener, the one who makes the gardens grow—gardens of the earth *and* of the heart. One seed . . . one day . . . at a time.

Sciatic Nerve Tumor–Summary/Lessons Learned

During the spring of 1995, about three and a half years after my ovarian cancer diagnosis, I was diagnosed with an inoperable, malignant tumor that was wrapped around my sciatic nerve. Six months before the second diagnosis I had been experiencing debilitating leg pain and pain in my buttocks. I went to my oncologist who ordered various tests to be done. Except for a couple of degenerative discs, the results of those tests came back normal. But the pain persisted and gradually got worse. I continued to pray for God's wisdom for the doctors and guidance for me. Six months later, after going from doctor to doctor, I was referred by my chiropractor to a doctor at the University of Minnesota. After a normal exam by that doctor, he called my oncologist and suggested that she order another MRI for me. He hinted at the possibility of a pelvic tumor.

My oncologist ordered the MRI and the results revealed a tumor wrapped around my sciatic nerve. I then underwent a needle biopsy to determine if it was cancerous or not.

It proved to be cancer. I then underwent radiation followed by six months of chemotherapy. Thankfully, I didn't get as sick from those chemotherapy treatments as I had during my ovarian cancer treatments. Through it all, I continued trusting my Heavenly Father, and through it all He was again faithful . . . supplying all that I needed to endure another cancer diagnosis.

One way that God helped me to endure my sciatic nerve tumor was by inspiring me with songs. I had tried writing songs before, but it had usually been a struggle putting the words and music together. During my second cancer, the words and music just flowed. The inspired songs fresh from God kept my focus heavenly. They blessed my life in a huge way. They were priceless gifts from God that he used to strengthen and encourage me during that time.

During my second cancer, God brought more truths, more lessons into my life. Looking back, seven stand out to me . . .

1. God may choose to give us His perspective on our situation if we ask Him for it. After I was diagnosed with my sciatic nerve tumor I asked God for His perspective on my situation. Over and over, He drew my attention to the gospel of John, Chapter 9, the story of a man who had been born blind. As Jesus and His disciples walked along, they saw a man who had been born blind. The disciples asked Jesus a question: "Rabbi, who sinned, this man or his parents, that he was born blind?" "Neither this man nor his parents sinned," said Jesus, "but this happened so that the work of God might be displayed in his life" (John 9:2–3, NIV). And Jesus healed the blind man. Using that story, God made it clear to me that, through my cancer, His work would be displayed and that I, like the blind man, would be healed . . . once again. Since that time, I have asked God many times for His perspective on various situations in my life. There's nothing like knowing His perspective.

2. I learned that God can work through any doctor and that He alone is the Great Physician. During my second bout with cancer, my gynecologist and surgeon from my ovarian

cancer left his practice. The day I found out that he would no longer be my doctor, I panicked. He knew everything about my history, and I felt sick to my stomach just thinking about it. But God was at work. The day after I learned about my gynecologist, I ran into his nurse when we were out boating (on a lake we rarely went to). I shared with her my feelings over losing my doctor and then asked her what doctor she would recommend for me to go to. She told me about another woman doctor in that same practice who she believed was very competent. After my conversation with the nurse that day, God made it clear to me that He can work through *any* doctor, and He revealed that I had been placing too much of my trust in a single doctor and not in Him alone. He reminded me that He alone is the Great Physician. I have never forgotten that lesson.

3. I learned that God's grace is sufficient and will always see me through. After my second cancer diagnosis, I told God that I needed His grace to see me through. Memories of my ovarian cancer were fresh in my mind. God lovingly reassured me through a nurse named Grace, that His grace was sufficient and would see me through, which it did. And since then, I have experienced over and over again the sufficiency of His grace. I know that it will *always* see me through, no matter what I encounter on my journey home.

4. I learned that sometimes God speaks to us through others in our lives. When my friends advised me to find another oncologist for my sciatic nerve tumor, I didn't take their advice seriously. But then I found myself in a dilemma.

My two doctors didn't agree on the treatment plan I should undergo. When I prayed for guidance God directed me to a new oncologist. My friends had been right all along. After that time, I began to seek the wise counsel of other Christians in my life, knowing that God might speak to me through them.

5. God will reveal His plan for our lives if we ask Him. Jeremiah 29:11 says, "For I know the plans I have for you," says the Lord. "They are plans for good and not for evil, to give you a future and a hope." Trusting God's Word to me, I knew that I would survive my second cancer. God was sparing my life a second time, and I wanted to know His plans for me. So I began to ask Him in prayer to reveal them. Eventually, He made it clear to me. I was to be a light of His love and His truth to the world around me. He revealed those plans for me through the Bible, through others, through prayer and even through music I was listening to during that time. I had lived thirty-seven years and hadn't known until my second cancer what God's plan for my life was. Knowing God's plan for my life has helped to keep me focused in a distracting world and has filled my life with even greater meaning and purpose.

6. I learned the importance of accepting my circumstances rather than fighting them. By accepting my circumstances (a second cancer diagnosis), I felt such freedom and felt empowered to move on and ask—*what now?* Instead of getting stuck in anger and bitterness—a dead-end street I didn't want to live on.

7. I learned to gratefully accept my healing. I've known a lot of people over the years—family, friends and acquaintances, who have died from cancer. There were times when I actually felt guilty that I had survived and they hadn't. One day I realized that guilt was robbing me of the joy of God's gift of healing, and I began choosing thanksgiving instead.

By God's grace I survived another cancer diagnosis, and for that I am forever grateful. God had more lessons for me to learn and more things to demonstrate through my life. I grew to know and love Him even more during my second cancer as I experienced His tender mercies and grace through it all. Even grace with skin on . . . (See Part 2, *Radiation and the Nurse.*)

Part Three
(Colon Cancer)

Perfect Timing

*He will keep in perfect peace all those who trust
in Him, whose thoughts turn often to the Lord!
(Isaiah 26:3)*

Perfect timing, I thought to myself after I discovered blood in
my stool only minutes before leaving for a routine appointment with my oncologist, Dr. Bowers. I knew then that I
would have to tell Dr. Bowers about it first thing.

On the way to my oncology appointment, Psalm 50:15
came to mind. It was the same verse that had been coming to
my mind that whole week. "I want you to trust me in your
times of trouble, so I can rescue you, and you can give me
glory." I wondered then why that verse came to me again on
the way to my appointment. What was God saying? I wasn't
sure, but I would wait expectantly for an answer.

The drive to Dr. Bowers' office went quickly, and soon I
was in the exam room waiting. When Dr. Bowers entered the
room, we greeted each other. "I just had a scary thing happen
to me as I was getting ready to come here today," I told her. She
asked me what had happened, and I told her about the blood

in my stool. "Well, we'll just have to check it out right away," she said, and then she ordered a CT scan and colonoscopy.

The CT scan was scheduled for the following week, and my meeting with a colon and rectal specialist was scheduled for the week after that. I left Dr. Bower's office that day unsure of what lay ahead, but thankful for family and friends I could count on once again to cover me in prayer.

Later that night, I read my Bible before going to bed. I read from Isaiah chapter 26. My eyes instantly fell on verses 3 and 4 because they were underlined. "He will keep in perfect peace all those who trust in Him, whose thoughts turn often to the Lord! Trust in the Lord God always, for in the Lord Jehovah is your everlasting strength."

Yes! The Lord was my strength and would be my strength . . . my everlasting strength. God spoke to me personally through those verses, and I felt His presence and peace enfolding me that night. God was speaking, and I was listening.

I knew that with God's help, I could stay focused on Him and not my upcoming scan and colonoscopy. He had seen me through so much already, and I trusted then that He would continue to see me through . . . one day at a time. I approached the throne of grace that night and left my burdens of the day there before falling fast asleep. Waiting for tests was nothing new . . .

Two Words From Above

I want you to trust me in your times of trouble,
so I can rescue you, and you can give me glory.
(Psalm 50:15)

With faithful family and friends surrounding me, I was covered in prayer while I waited to have the two tests Dr. Bowers had ordered for me, a CT scan and a colonoscopy. I felt God's presence daily through prayer, His word, and the love of family and friends. I knew He was listening to the cry of our hearts. The days went by quicky, and before I knew it, my CT scan was behind me. I praised God that the scan had gone smoothly without complications.

The following week was my scheduled appointment with Dr. Finney, the colon and rectal specialist. When fear threatened to overwhelm me on the days between my CT scan and the meeting with Dr. Finney (who I assumed was going to do the colonoscopy), I repeated Isaiah 26:3–4 to myself over and over until peace filled my heart and left no room for fear. "He will keep in perfect peace all those who trust in Him, whose thoughts turn often to the Lord! Trust in the Lord God always, for in the Lord Jehovah is your everlasting strength."

The day finally arrived for my appointment with Dr. Finney, and Pete accompanied me to that appointment. When we arrived at Dr. Finney's office, there was a short wait before we were brought into his office. After meeting him, he reviewed my chart and asked several questions.

"You had a colonoscopy nine months ago, and I really don't see any reason to do another one now if that one was normal," Dr. Finney told us. "We usually do them every five years if they turn out normal." This meant that I wouldn't need a colonoscopy for five years.

While Dr. Finney spoke, two words popped into my mind like a bolt of lightening. I immediately sensed that God was at work sending me those two words from above. The two words that interrupted my thoughts were, flexible sigmoidoscopy. "Is a flexible sigmoidoscopy the same as a colonoscopy?" I asked Dr. Finney. "No," Dr. Finney answered. "Well, I think I had a flexible sigmoidoscopy nine months ago, not a colonoscopy." Dr. Finney thought for a moment and then said, "In that case, we should do a colonoscopy considering your family history of colon cancer." The colonoscopy was scheduled for two weeks later.

By the time we left Dr. Finney's office that day I knew that God had given me the two words, for a reason. I left that appointment wondering why. Maybe there was a polyp, maybe something else. I was convinced then that something was in my colon that needed to be checked out.

I dreaded the thought of a colonoscopy. The flexible sigmoidoscopy had been incredibly painful for me, and I had been told that the colonoscopy involved an even longer scope so that more of the colon could be viewed. I couldn't do the colonoscopy in my own strength. I prayed and I prayed, asking for God's strength to see me through.

I dug into God's Word at that time, too, bracing myself for the fiery arrows that I knew my enemy, Satan, would begin shooting at me days prior to my colonoscopy. Psalm 50:15 came to me as I waited for my colonoscopy, just as it had when I discovered blood in my stool: "I want you to trust me in your times of trouble, so I can rescue you, and you can give me glory." God was definitely calling me to trust, but what was He specifically calling me to trust Him for? I didn't know for sure, but my mind kept wondering. Was it a third bout with cancer I'd be trusting Him for? Only time would tell.

Saved From My Enemies

All I need to do is cry to Him—Oh, praise the Lord—and I am saved from all my enemies! (Psalm 18:3)

The morning of my scheduled colonoscopy, before Pete and I left for the hospital, I read my devotions. That morning, I happened to turn to John chapter 9. John 9 is the story of the blind man who was healed by Jesus. Physical ailments back then were thought to have been brought on by sin. In John 9, the disciples questioned Jesus regarding the man's blindness: "Rabbi, who sinned, this man or his parents, that he was born blind?" "Neither this man nor his parents sinned," said Jesus, "but this happened so that the work of God might be displayed in his life" (John 9:2–3, NIV).

After reading John 9 that morning, my thoughts turned to my second cancer. I had prayed and prayed for God's perspective after my second cancer diagnosis. What came to me over and over at that time through Christian radio shows, church, Bible reading and prayer was John 9 . . . the same story I read that morning before my colonoscopy.

During my second cancer, I had known that I would survive because God had given me His perspective through His Word. I remembered God's faithfulness to me back then and the fact that He cannot lie. I also remembered then how God's power truly had been demonstrated through my second cancer.

After this flashback on the morning of my colonoscopy, I returned to my Bible. I read John chapter 10, and following that passage in my devotional Bible was Psalm 116. Again, my thoughts were stirred. Memories of my first cancer flashed on the screen of my mind.

God had used Psalm 116 when I had ovarian cancer to assure me that I would survive. Psalm 116:9 says, "I shall live! Yes, in His presence—here on earth!"

God spoke to me so clearly the morning of my colonoscopy through John 9 and Psalm 116. I was convinced after reading them and meditating on them that no matter what lay ahead, I would survive and God's power would be demonstrated.

With my morning devotions behind me, I got ready. Pete and I then left for the hospital. Soon I found myself in the main waiting room of the office where I was scheduled to have the colonoscopy. Pete offered the newspaper to me while we waited, but I declined. Instead, I pulled out a folded piece of paper from my pocket. I had written down several Bible verses to help me stay focused on the Lord while we waited that morning. I unfolded the piece of paper and scanned the following:

All I need to do is cry to Him—oh, praise the Lord—and I am saved from all my enemies! (Psalm 18:3)

But I will always trust in you and in your mercy and shall rejoice in your salvation. (Psalm 13:5)

Listen to my pleading, Lord! Be merciful and send the help I need. (Psalm 27:7)

For I cried to Him and He answered me! He freed me from all my fears. (Psalm 34:4)

The Lord takes care of those He has forgiven. (Psalm 37:17b)

Give your burdens to the Lord. He will carry them. He will not permit the godly to slip or fall. (Psalm 55:22)

He will give His people strength. He will bless them with peace. (Psalm 29:11)

But when I am afraid, I will put my confidence in you. Yes, I will trust the promises of God. And since I am trusting Him, what can mere man do to me? (Psalm 56:3–4)

Your kindness and love are as vast as the heavens. Your faithfulness is higher than the skies. (Psalm 57:10)

O God, have pity, for I am trusting You! I will hide beneath the shadow of your wings until this storm is past. (Psalm 57:1)

He is close to all who call on Him sincerely. He fulfills the desires of those who reverence and trust Him; He hears their cries for help and rescues them. (Psalm 145:18–19)

He does not ignore the prayers of men in trouble when they call to Him for help. (Psalm 9:12b)

Of all the verses on the list, Psalm 18:3 stood out for me and comforted me the most. "All I need to do is cry to Him— oh, praise the Lord—and I am saved from all my enemies!" I read that verse over and over until I had it memorized. I then did what the verse suggested—I called on the Lord to save me from my enemies, my enemies of fear and doubt that had been trying to gain victory over me all morning. Soon, while still waiting for my name to be called, the Lord replaced those enemies with His strength.

Memories of the painful sigmoidoscopy I had experienced nine months earlier kept trying to destroy my welcomed peace and strength from above. So I repeated to myself over and over the fact that God would see me through, God would see me through.

"Tamara Windahl," the nurse announced. Pete and I got up from our chairs and followed her. The minute my eyes met that nurse's eyes I felt covered with unbelievable love and compassion. She escorted us to a room where she took my vitals and gave me a gown to change into.

I went to the restroom to change into a gown, and before leaving the restroom, I knelt down. I felt fear rising again, and so I called on the Lord again, to save me from my enemies.

After praying, I returned to the room where Pete and the nurse were waiting for me. It was then that I spelled out my concerns to the loving nurse, who I was convinced was an instrument of Jesus' love to me that day. I told her how painful my last flexible sigmoidoscopy had been. "I don't think this will be as bad for you," she reassured me. She told me they'd give me something for pain, and if it wasn't enough, I could just ask for more.

Shortly thereafter, Dr. Finney was ready to perform the colonoscopy. I was given some pain medication, but it wasn't enough, so I requested more, thankful for the nurse's earlier advice.

During the exam, I thought I heard Dr. Finney say, "There's a tumor . . ." but I wasn't positive.

After the procedure, the nurse wheeled me back to a room. The nurse mentioned that they had moved me from my original room because someone else had needed it.

As the nurse wheeled me into the new room, I looked out the large window in front of me. The only thing I saw as I looked out the window was a cross on a church in the distance. It was as if I were looking at one of those hidden pictures and the cross jumped right out at me. It seemed that the cross on that church was the only thing in my view.

"Look what's out there . . . the cross on that church!" I exclaimed. She smiled and said that I wouldn't have seen it if they hadn't moved me to the new room. God was indeed near. I felt His love surrounding me and helping me to keep a heavenly focus.

After the nurse got me situated, the doctor joined us. With a serious face, he broke the news to us. He indeed had seen a tumor in my colon. He believed, though, that they could remove it all through surgery. Cancer number three . . .

Although I was sad upon hearing Dr. Finney's announcement, I wasn't surprised. For I truly had suspected that something was wrong with me after my initial appointment with him. Why else would God have given me the words "flexible sigmoidoscopy" during that meeting?

The unknown finally became known that day. There's something to be said about knowing . . . even if it's bad news.

I was so thankful then that God had given me those two words from above. Without those two words, I would not have had a colonoscopy for five more years. The tumor would have gone undiagnosed . . .

On the way home from the hospital with Pete at my side, my thoughts returned to my devotions from earlier that morning. Meditating on those two passages, I was again comforted.

While Pete drove, my mind continued to wander. Not to scary places, but to more Scripture. Psalm 50:15 was the next verse that came to mind, "I want you to trust me in your times of trouble, so I can rescue you, and you can give me glory." God's repeated message to me through Psalm 50:15 brought added comfort and indomitable strength. I understood then why the Lord had kept drawing me to it. Yes! It was true! I would survive the colon cancer—by the grace of God on the wings of faith. I needed to trust God. He would rescue me, and when He did, I would give Him all the glory by shouting it from the mountaintop. The same mountaintop where I had been before, after my first cancer and my second cancer . . .

By the time Pete and I arrived home that afternoon from my colonoscopy, I was exhausted. Yet, at the same time, I was filled with God's amazing peace, the peace "which surpasses all understanding." (Philippians 4:7, NRSV)

God had trained me well in the crucible of cancer number one and cancer number two. I knew then that by His grace I would continue to trust Him, and by His grace I would focus on the cross—not on the rest of the picture. For God had spoken. He would rescue me. No doubt about it.

Enemies and Mountains

Here on earth you will have many trials and sorrows; but cheer up, for I have overcome the world. (John 16:33)

Shortly before I found out that I had colon cancer I had started reading *Hinds Feet on High Places* by Hannah Hurnard. The book had been recommended by a Bible study leader years earlier. Even though I had bought the book back then, I had never read the whole thing. I had actually started reading it more than once but just couldn't get into it. For a long time it sat, unread, on our bookshelf. Then one day before my colon cancer diagnosis, it caught my eye. I took it off the shelf once more, wiped a layer of dust off it and decided to try reading it again.

Hinds Feet on High Places is an allegory (a story in which people, things, and happenings have a hidden meaning) about the Christian's journey through life. The main character is on a journey to the "high places." As she begins the journey, her friend, the Shepherd, introduces her to her traveling companions: sorrow and suffering. And he tells her, "Whenever you call for help, I promise to come to you at once."

While on their journey, the main character and her companions encounter many enemies and difficulties, but one thing is certain. Whenever the main character calls for the Shepherd, he comes. The main character is tempted at times to quit her journey and to go back home, but she doesn't. She trusts the Shepherd and his promises and eventually reaches the "high places." Once there, she realizes the journey, though difficult, was worth it.

I was about halfway through reading the book when I found out that I had colon cancer. Within days of hearing my diagnosis, I picked up *Hinds Feet on High Places* again.

Reading one day, the Shepherd's words to the main character at the beginning of the book as she began her journey came to me: "Whenever you call for help, I promise to come to you at once." Thinking about the Shepherd's words, I realized how similar his words were to the words of Psalm 18:3, the verse God had so clearly spoken to me through on the day of my colonoscopy and the days following: "All I need to do is cry to Him—oh, praise the Lord—and I am saved from all my enemies!"

I then thought about how I, like the book's main character, needed only to call on Him. I also considered then how the Shepherd in the book had chased away enemies, and I realized how God had daily been chasing away my enemies when I called on Him. God was indeed at work, wonderfully weaving things together to reveal Himself and to teach me new lessons—lessons I knew would be life-changing and unforgettable when taught by my Heavenly Father.

I was convinced that somehow, supernaturally, God had placed *Hinds Feet on High Places* in my hands at that moment in time. He knew what I would be going through then and how that book would encourage me to continue on my own faith journey, just like the main character in the book, instead of turning back.

After contemplating God's incredible ways that day, I felt Him wonderfully near. I was reminded then that He was accompanying me up the mountain. And although the terrain on my mountain path had grown rocky, I trusted that He would see me through—both before and after my scheduled surgery. The surgery would be just another resting place on my way up the mountain.

P.S. Remembering *Hinds Feet on High Places*, I'm reminded of the main character's struggle, which in turn reminds me of my own. The Holy Spirit then reminds me of Jesus' words in John 16:33, "Here on earth you will have many trials and sorrows; but cheer up, for I have overcome the world." This world certainly is full of troubles, but Jesus *has* overcome the world. It is *He* who goes *before* me and *with* me each step of my journey here on earth. He strengthens me each day for that day's climb up the mountain to the mountaintop. The mountaintop where one day (like the main character in *Hinds Feet on High Places*), I will be all God wants me to be. Where one day I, too, will know without a shadow of a doubt that my journey on earth, though difficult, was worth it. And then . . . let the party begin!

Crosses and Rainbows

For just as the heavens are higher than the earth, so are my ways higher than yours, and my thoughts than yours. (Isaiah 55:9)

The days before my colon cancer surgery were packed with things to get done. Sunday, though, was reserved for worship and an afternoon of boating. At the time, I felt that this Sunday would most likely be my last time boating for the 1998 season. Before Pete, Zach, our friend Jen and I left for the lake, I prayed for God's special blessing on our day together.

It was a glorious summer day in Minnesota that Sunday, and our afternoon was blessed with laughter and fun. I truly sensed God's special blessing in answer to my earlier prayer.

On the way back to the marina, Zach and Jen were on the skibob, bouncing on the waves behind the boat, having a blast. All of a sudden, an alarm for the boat's oil gauge went off. Pete slowed down, told the kids to climb into the boat and then headed back to the marina . . . slowly.

On our way back to the marina, a deep sadness came over me. *How many of these people out here have to have surgery on Wednesday?!* I silently questioned in a state of self-pity, my newest enemy to appear. With that question bobbing in my mind, I quickly called on God for His strength as the words of Psalm 18:3 came to mind, "All I need to do is cry to Him— oh, praise the Lord—and I am saved from all my enemies!"

After calling on God, I happened to glance backwards. Scanning the lake, I spotted two boats in the distance—

sailboats with their sails down. I was still watching those two boats when, all of a sudden, it was as if my mind forgot that they were sailboats and instead saw them as two large crosses standing on the water. I sat in silence. God had heard my prayer amidst the waves in the water and in my soul, and He was clearly answering. I was awestruck at what He was providing for me—special delivery out on the lake, "crosses." Crosses were a simple reminder to focus on Him. I turned back around in my seat on the boat overcome with joy, for my spiritual vision had been restored.

I glanced back a second time to marvel at the crosses once again, and saw something else amazing. Tiny waves behind the boat caught my eyes, tiny waves that wouldn't have been there if Zach and Jen had still been on the skibob.

As the tiny waves danced in the sunshine, small rainbows were produced all around the back of the boat—all around *me*. Since becoming a believer and reading about God's gift of a rainbow to Noah and the world in Genesis 9, I haven't looked at rainbows quite the same. Rainbows had come to remind me that God's promises are true. With my eyes focused on the many rainbows around the boat—around *me*—I was reminded of God's faithfulness and His specific promise to never leave me.

Self-pity was sent scurrying as my thoughts were transformed. My new thoughts silently announced . . . *how amazing, how awesome, how good is my God!* When I call to Him, He comes and saves me from my enemies—no matter where I am—lakeside, seaside, bedside, wherever. And He will never leave me. Never. Ever.

Riding back the last stretch to the marina, my traveling companions had no idea of the battle and victory that had taken place in my mind. Silently, I praised God for His strength, for His promises and for His love. Two sailboats and some tiny waves had brought comfort and strength just days before surgery. Talk about God's amazing ways! His simply amazing ways . . .

Anointed with Oil

He is my strength and song in the heat of battle, and now He has given me the victory. (Psalm 118:14)

David shouted in reply "You come to me with a sword and a spear, but I come to you in the name of the Lord of the armies of heaven and of Israel—the very God whom you have defied. Today the Lord will conquer you. (1 Samuel 17:45–46)

My colon cancer surgery was two days away, and I knew that the closer I got to surgery the more intense the battle would be against my enemies of fear and doubt. I knew that I needed to do all I could to prepare for their attacks.

During that time, Psalm 18:3 still came to mind over and over again, "All I need to do is cry to Him—oh, praise the Lord—and I am saved from all my enemies!" So, daily, I called on the Lord through prayer, spent time in God's Word and praised Him.

When I woke up Tuesday, the day before surgery, I reached for my Bible and happened to read Psalm 118. Verse 14 stood out: "He is my strength and song in the heat of battle, and now He has given me the victory." God spoke to me so clearly through that verse, and I was strengthened. He was my strength and would bring me victory.

Hebrews 4:12 describes God's Word as "living and active"(NIV). I experienced the truth of that verse daily. I don't know how I could have made it through each day without His personal messages to me through His "living" Word.

After hearing God's message to me for that day through Psalm 118, I took a shower. While in the shower, a song played in my mind, "God Is So Good."

After I showered, I ate breakfast and checked my calendar for the day. I needed to be at church at eleven o'clock that morning for a prayer session a friend had arranged for me. Several friends would be there to pray, along with available staff from our church. James 5:14 says, "Is anyone sick? He should call for the elders of the church and they should pray over Him and pour a little oil upon Him, calling on the Lord to heal Him." I was sick and we were following the Bible's instructions on what to do.

I arrived at church shortly before eleven o'clock and found friends and staff gathering to pray. When everyone arrived, we went into a room just outside the senior pastor's office. I was told I would be anointed with oil and that the others would lay hands on me as prayers were offered.

Our pastor said that he wanted to begin by reading Psalm 118—unaware that Psalm 118 was the same Scripture God had already used to strengthen me during my earlier morning devotions! God was clearly at work.

Psalm 118 begins, "Give thanks to the Lord, for He is good; his love endures forever" (NIV). As our pastor read that verse, the song from my morning shower came to mind, "God Is So Good."

These verses stood out for me as the pastor continued reading the Psalm. Verse 8 says, "It is better to trust the Lord than to put confidence in men." Verse 14 says, "He is my strength and song in the heat of battle, and now He has given me the victory." Verse 17 says, "I shall not die, but live to tell of all His deeds." God was again speaking through Psalm 118, and I was listening. Intently listening.

The Bible says in Matthew 18:20, "For where two or three gather together because they are mine, I will be right there among them." We knew God was with us that morning of the prayer session, and an incredible sense of strength, power, love and peace filled the room. One by one, people offered praise, thanksgiving and prayers for peace, comfort and God's healing touch for me. We were before the throne of God, and we knew that He was listening.

In closing our prayer session, our pastor suggested we sing the doxology together. I asked him if we could instead sing the song that had been playing in my mind that whole week. I said that I didn't remember all of the words but that one of the verses spoke of being "saved from my enemies." He graciously suggested that I should just start singing it and that someone would know it. The words to the song "I Will

Call Upon the Lord" by Michael L. O' Shields came flooding back to me as we all sang, and joy filled my heart . . .

I left church covered in prayers and love that day, full of the strength of the Lord. I felt as if *my* Goliath had just been defeated and would no longer be able to taunt me. God was at work giving me strength for battle and was indeed saving me from my enemies.

Led by the Spirit

If we are living now by the Holy Spirit's power, let us follow the Holy Spirit's leading in every part of our lives. (Galatians 5:25)

After the prayer session at church, I headed to the hospital to get a shot to raise my low white blood cell count (to help fight off infections) before surgery. My friend, Jeanne, along with Zach and his friend, Jimmy, went with me to the hospital.

At the hospital, I saw several of the nurses that had cared for me over the years. They were more than nurses, they were friends. When they saw me, they wanted to know what was happening with me. We spoke for some time before I got my shot and then said goodbye. As we were about to leave the hospital, I remembered I needed to make a call to my doctor's office before we left. Zach and Jimmy ran to get some food while I made the call. We ended up spending more time at the hospital than I had originally planned, but finally we were ready to leave.

Walking out the door of the hospital, we ran into Bonnie, one of the nurses who had cared for my dad a couple of months earlier. I stopped to talk to her while my buddies headed to the car. Bonnie wanted to know how Dad, who was suffering from liver cancer at the time, was doing. I filled her in and then told her that I was scheduled for surgery the next day myself. Bonnie is a Christian, and I told her I had just come from a prayer session for me at our church. She hugged me and said, "Jesus is on the throne." She then told me she'd be praying for me.

Before saying goodbye, Bonnie reached into her bag for something. "I don't know why I grabbed this this morning to bring to work, but I thought someone might need it today." With that, she handed me a cassette tape, a cassette tape of *healing* scripture songs—exactly what I would need after surgery!

It wasn't a coincidence that Jeanne, Zach, Jimmy and I had spent just the right amount of time at the hospital. Not too much . . . not too little . . . just enough so we would run into Bonnie on her way to work. It was all part of God's perfect plan for me that day.

Bonnie was guided by the Holy Spirit that morning to bring a cassette tape with her to work. She didn't know why, but she listened and obeyed the Holy Spirit's prompting anyway. Because of her obedience, I was blessed. Through her actions, I felt God's touch and His love.

On the way to the car with Bonnie's cassette tape in my hand, I was totally overcome with emotion, lost in the music of God's love for me. The whole way to the car I kept exclaiming, "Oohh! Oohhh!" I felt overwhelming joy and praise. Like King David in the Old Testament, I felt like dancing for the Lord.

Jeanne, Zach and Jimmy were waiting at the car for me. I relayed the story of Bonnie and the tape. They were touched by God, too. Excitement and praise filled the car as we drove home.

That night, I thought about Bonnie and her obedience to the Spirit's prompting. I realized anew the impact that my obedience to the Holy Spirit's promptings has on other people. I wondered how many others had missed out on a blessing from God because of my failure at times to listen to and then obey the Spirit's promptings. I imagined what the world would look like if Christians everywhere were totally guided by the Holy Spirit every day. If this were truly the case, God would no longer be like one of those hidden pictures so popular several years ago. Instead, He would clearly be seen through the lives of believers. I pictured in my mind what a beautiful picture that would be. A possible picture? Yes! A probable picture? Probably not in today's world of endless distractions.

That night, while contemplating that beautiful picture of Christians being guided by the Holy Spirit, I grew even more determined to paint my part of that picture daily. I prayed that I would be led by the Holy Spirit each and every day. On my part of the picture, I wanted God to clearly shine through, instead of being hidden behind sins of selfishness, pride and greed. It was much food for thought the night before surgery.

Mountains

I Lift My Eyes Up

I lift my eyes up
Up to the mountain.
Where does my help come from?
My help comes from you,
Maker of heaven,
Creator of the earth.
(Brian Doerksen)

Have you ever noticed how God uses anything and everything at times to reveal Himself to us and to teach us new lessons? Well, after a successful surgery for colon cancer, God continued to speak to me about mountains.

One day after surgery, alone in my hospital room, I glanced at the table next to me and spotted a card from one of my friends. The card had a simple drawing on it, and while looking at it then, it was as if I were seeing it for the first time. On the front of the card was a goat on a mountain, which reminded me of the cover of the book *Hinds Feet on High Places*, the book God had been using so mightily in my life at that time. After studying the card for a short time, I spotted a note alongside it. The note was from Pete, saying that his cousins (which I consider my cousins!) and their families had prayed for me, on top of . . . what else?! . . . a mountain!

I thought of the theme of enemies and mountains that God had been using in my life at that time. I considered anew how everything that had happened to me, including cancer, was all part of my journey up the mountain.

Through a simple drawing on a card and a note from Pete, I was reminded that God was near and that He would continue to strengthen me and help me on my journey up the mountain. I was comforted again by knowing that my journey was not a solo endeavor.

While still in the hospital, Pete's cousins came to visit me—the ones who had prayed for me on top of that mountain during their vacation. They brought me a gift that brought tears to my eyes. It was a hand-carved bowl by Pete's cousin, Tammy. In the bowl were three hand-painted rocks and a pinecone. The word "faith" was painted on one of the rocks, "hope" on another and "love" on the remaining one. Each rock came from a different mountain, and on the bottom of the bowl, Tammy had written from which mountains they had come.

They also brought along a map that evening and showed me exactly where the mountain was where they had prayed for me. God's "mountain" theme in my life continued.

When I got home from my week-long hospital stay following surgery, another amazing thing happened. One night, after finding out earlier that day that Dad's cancer was advancing and that he was in the hospital again, I felt sad. I was still weak and recovering from my own surgery. My burden was so great that I cried out to God, once again for His strength and for Him to "save me from my enemies."

After that silent heart cry to God, my family and I began watching a favorite TV show. The story that night involved a young woman who was a drug addict. She was an artist, and before her addiction she had painted scenes of . . . what else?! . . . mountains! I was speechless as beautiful paintings of mountains appeared on the screen. I sat glued to the TV set. Near the end of the show, the drug addict character decided to go through withdrawal from drugs with the help of an angel. It was an incredibly difficult time, and an angel told the girl something like, "Keep your eyes on the top of the mountain—He is there." Those words were comforting words for my own soul.

In one scene, the young woman dreamt of ascending the mountain with the angel's help. When they reached the top, a beautiful landscape full of light emerged, and it seemed to me to be symbolic of the glory of the Lord surrounding them.

My heart overflowed with praise. God had heard my prayer for His strength that night and had answered me using a TV show. A show that reminded me once again that He was indeed near and would continue helping me ascend the mountain on my journey of faith—no matter how steep the incline was.

Looking back on my "mountain" lessons during my colon cancer, I'm reminded of God's promise in Jeremiah 29:13, "You will seek me and find me when you seek me with all your heart"(NIV). I *was* wholeheartedly seeking God back then, and I'm still in awe of the ways He clearly revealed Himself to me. First and foremost through His Word, but, also, through a book, a card, a note, a gift and even a TV show.

Over the course of my faith journey, I have learned that I must take time daily to be still and to listen to God. Not only in the valleys of life, but, also on the mountaintops. For He has so very much to say to me about mountains, enemies and so much more. And although I don't as of yet know what my next classes will be, one thing is for certain: I know my teacher and He knows me, including the lessons I still need to learn on my way on up—the mountain.

Colon Cancer–Summary/Lessons Learned

My colon cancer was another test of my faith. It was another opportunity to put my faith into action and to witness God's amazing ways. Over and over, God revealed to me during that time that He was going to heal me . . . again. I marveled and still marvel at His unfathomable mercy and grace in my life.

For colon cancer, I underwent major surgery. The doctors removed three quarters of my colon. My surgery was a success as far as removing all of the cancer, and I didn't need to undergo chemotherapy or radiation. For that, I was so very thankful.

During my colon cancer, God's presence was clearly evident to me again. He clearly revealed Himself over and over, always at just the right time. Knowing He was near gave me strength to continue on.

During this time, God directed me time and again to Psalm 50:15, "I want you to trust me in your times of trouble, so I can rescue you, and you can give me glory." By His grace, I chose to do my part according to that verse. I trusted God and gave Him the glory when He rescued me. And God did His part. He rescued me; He healed me. His miracles continued. As I look back, two specific lessons come to mind that God taught me during colon cancer.

1. I learned that fear, doubt, self-pity and discouragement are real enemies of mine. I discovered this through a book God had directed me to read. I had never considered fear and doubt as actual "enemies" before. Seeing them as enemies shed a whole new light on them, and I began to look out for them every day. I was determined not to let them steal my joy!

2. I learned that when I call on the Lord, He comes and saves me from my enemies. God directed me over and over again to Psalm 18:3, "All I need to do is cry to Him—oh, praise the Lord—and I am saved from all my enemies!" The book God directed me to read had a similar thought. The Shepherd, who represents Jesus, tells the main character, "Whenever you call for help I promise to come to you at once." When I began to recognize the specific enemies in my life—fear, doubt, self-pity and others—I would immediately call out to Jesus, just as Psalm 18:3 had directed me to do. Sometimes I called out verbally, other times I called in silent prayer: "Jesus, help!" And Jesus never let me down. He always came. He always saved me from my enemies.

God was true to his word to me, and I survived a third bout with cancer. I am speechless when I consider all that He has done for me.

Within a span of seven months, my family and I experienced the following:

1. My dad underwent many medical procedures and was ultimately diagnosed with liver cancer.
2. Dad moved in with us for a while because of his illness.
3. Dad was forced to sell his house and car because of his illness.
4. We found an assisted living residence for Dad and moved him into it.
5. We sorted through Dad's house of more than forty years.
6. We arranged for a sale of Dad's things.
7. We brought Dad to many doctor's visits. He was hospitalized a few times.
8. I was diagnosed with colon cancer.
9. I had major surgery.
10. At one point, Dad and I both were hospitalized at the same time at different hospitals.
11. Sadly, Dad passed away after a short battle with cancer.
12. We cleaned out Dad's apartment.
13. We took care of Dad's financial and personal matters after his death.

I personally experienced the truth of the saying, "Life is hard, but God is good." There were many difficult days during that time. Yet God, in His goodness and mercy, supplied my needs, one day at a time, when I cried out to Him. Through the book I was reading at the time, God encouraged me not to give up but to continue trusting Him, even when I didn't understand His ways.

He reminded me during those hard days that I wasn't home yet, and that the best is yet to come. By His grace, I didn't give up but continued trusting Him. Psalm 86:5 says, "O Lord, you are so good and kind, so ready to forgive; so full of mercy for all who ask your aid." Psalm 136:1 says, "Oh, give thanks to the Lord, for He is good; His lovingkindness continues forever." And 1 John 2:29 tells us that, "God is always good and does only right." Yes, life is hard, but God is good. Always . . . always . . . good.

Part Four
(Breast Cancer)

Do Not Be Afraid

Be strong and courageous! Do not be afraid or discouraged. For the Lord your God is with you wherever you go. *(Joshua 1:9, NLT)*

In November 1999, I read an article in a Christian magazine about a little boy who had experienced a house fire and had placed his faith in God's promise given in Joshua 1:9 (see above). Not only was Joshua 1:9 referred to in the magazine article, but it was also highlighted in a box at the end of the article. What a great verse, I thought to myself. Then I ripped out the page with the highlighted verse on it, determined to memorize it with Zach. Joshua 1:9 remained on my mind days after reading that article.

A short time later, in early December, I read Psalm 147:11, "But His joy is in those who reverence Him, those who expect Him to be loving and kind." Just like Joshua 1:9 had stayed on my mind, Psalm 147:11 did, too.

Psalm 147:11 and Joshua 1:9 were on my mind daily when God brought another verse to mind: "Be still and know that I am God"(Psalm 46:10, NIV). Although it was a busy time, just weeks before Christmas, I slowed down in obedience to God's command by taking even more time than usual in my daily quiet time with Him. During those quiet times, I began to hear God whisper, "Do not be afraid," the same message as Joshua 1:9.

Another "do not be afraid" message came to me while at our last scheduled Bible study at church just before Christmas. As our small group time came to a close, Janet, a member of our group, told us that she was feeling dizzy. We all gathered around her and joined in prayer. Afterwards, a member of our group pointed to a board in the room where we were meeting. There was a message from the kids' program that same week. Janet, along with the rest of us, looked at the board and read, "Do not be afraid." As soon as I read it I sensed the message was for me, not Janet. I just didn't understand then why God was telling me over and over to not be afraid. It just didn't make sense to me at all.

Days later, I got a call from the doctor's office regarding the results of a mammogram I had taken a month before. I was told I needed a second mammogram because they had seen an abnormality on the first one. God's "message" started to make sense . . .

The day before my second mammogram, the following words stood out to me during the sermon at our church that Sunday, "God always leaves a space—an opportunity to trust God for the unknown. We often have unanswered questions, doubts, uncertainties like Joseph." I, like Joseph, would trust God, I thought to myself. Regardless of what lay ahead.

After a second mammogram, the doctor ordered a needle biopsy because at that point she couldn't rule out cancer.

Leaving the doctor's office that day, the "do not be afraid" message played in my mind. And I chose then, with God's help, to not be afraid.

The day after that second mammogram, Isaiah 41:10 from my morning devotions stood out to me. "Do not fear, for I am with you, do not be afraid, for I am your God. I will strengthen you, I will help you, I will uphold you with my victorious right hand" (NRSV). My heart danced after reading it because that was the verse God had given me during my sciatic nerve tumor to assure me that I would survive.

As I waited for the day of the needle biopsy procedure, God's words filled my mind. "Do not be afraid." With God's help, I wasn't afraid. I was truly at peace, and my heart was full of expectation. I expected God—even more than usual—to be loving and kind, just as Psalm 147:11 had instructed me.

A week before the needle biopsy, I spoke out of town at a Christian women's luncheon. A Christian trio sang for us, and on my way out the door after the luncheon, a member of that trio gave me one of their tapes. On the highway, heading home, I popped that tape in the tape player, anxious to hear more of the trio's music. As I listened, I felt God clearly speaking to me through one song in particular:

I will go before you, steadfast to the end,
I will walk beside you, closer than a friend,
I have pledged to uphold you, you are safe in my hand,
Do not fear, I am near, staying by your side.
Do not fear, I am here, I promise to abide.
I will go before you, faithfully endure

Angels now surround you, you may rest assured
I the Lord God have spoken
You are safe and secure
Do not fear, I am near, staying by your side
Do not fear, I am here, I promise to abide.

I am here, do not fear, I will stay with you
I am here, do not fear, I will be with you.

(David J. Schut)

When the song was over, a shiver of fear went through me. Did I really have cancer again? Cancer #4?! As I pondered that possibility, God's words came to me again. "Do not be afraid." Looking back over the previous weeks, I was amazed at God's incredible methods for getting that message across to me.

God's instruction to not be afraid was definitely loud and clear! I was so thankful then that He had urged me to slow down the weeks before Christmas and that by His grace I had obeyed. If I hadn't, I would have missed His comforting words to me, "do not be afraid," at a time when I needed them most.

Peace settled in once again as I made my way home, listening to the rest of that "God-given" tape ...

Victory

The day after the luncheon where I had received that God-given tape, I was vacuuming, getting our house ready for a Christmas party the following Monday night. While vacuuming the living room, I glanced over at the dining room floor that I had just vacuumed. It still looked really dusty to me, so I decided to clean it again when I finished vacuuming.

As I dusted the dining room floor, a light bulb went on in my mind. I remembered a TV commercial for the kind of cleaning instrument I was using then. On the commercial a woman was shown using that kind of cleaning instrument to clean under a refrigerator. I had never tried that before and, for some reason, I decided to give it a try. I went to the kitchen, slid the instrument under the refrigerator and pulled out some dust. I noticed something in the dust, and I looked closer. It was a magnetic word. Months earlier we had had a bunch of magnetic words (to make sentences out of) on the refrigerator. But I had taken them down because they kept falling off. I reached down and picked up the one word that had been left behind in the dust: "victory." I smiled to myself. My needle biopsy was the following week. "Victory" was a good word to find . . .

God's Truth and the Gynecologist

In the world you will have tribulation, but cheer up, for I have overcome the world. (John 16:33, NKJV)

On Saturday, the day after I found the magnetic "victory" word while cleaning, I felt a lot of pelvic pressure. Although the word "victory" kept coming to me throughout that weekend, I decided the following Monday I would make an appointment with a gynecologist.

On Sunday of that same weekend, the kids' choir at church sang a song, *My Deliverer is Coming*. Like the "victory" word, the words of that song stayed with me, too.

By Monday, I still had pelvic pressure, and I called my doctor's office. We had new insurance at the time, and I needed a doctor's referral for any visits to see a specialist, such as a gynecologist. Before we could get a referral, we had to see a regular doctor. On the phone with the doctor's office, I requested a referral to a gynecologist immediately. Otherwise, they would have first scheduled a regular doctor's visit for me. Surprisingly, they gave me a referral (which had to be an act of God!) over the phone. I was scheduled to see a new gynecologist the following Thursday.

After scheduling the appointment, fear started creeping in. But that night I read Jesus' words to Jairus in Mark 5:36— "Don't be afraid. Just trust me!" I felt God clearly speaking to me again. *Yes, I would trust,* I thought to myself. By Thursday, the day of my appointment, the pelvic pressure had subsided somewhat, but I kept the gynecological appointment anyway.

Before leaving for my appointment that morning, I read my devotions that included these words from John 16:33, "In the world you will have tribulation" (NKJV).

I also read these words: "With this great certainty and assurance the future holds no terrors we cannot face. Thus the Christian should never be filled with fear, discouragement, or despondency."

My dear sister-in-Christ, another Deb, accompanied me to my appointment with the new gynecologist. In the car on the way to that appointment, I told Deb the verse I had read that morning from John, "In the world you will have tribulation." I told her that I didn't like reading that right before my appointment. It seemed like a sign of things to come. Deb listened and then told me that what I had already been going through—the doctor's visits, medical tests, and so was a trial, a tribulation.

At the appointment, after giving my new gynecologist a brief health history, he asked me what type of cancer cell my ovarian cancer had been. I told him I didn't know. He left the room while I changed into an exam gown. When he returned, he told me he had made a phone call to obtain the information and then said, "Frankly, I can't believe you're here!" I told him it was a miracle, and he agreed.

While he prepared for my examination he asked, "Do you ever get mad at life?" Immediately I answered, "No, we're told that we'll suffer—have trials." He then asked me how I get through it all. I told him, "Faith, I couldn't do it without it."

After a good exam, I exclaimed, "Praise God! Praise God!" And I added, "You wouldn't believe all the prayers that have been said for you and for me." The doctor didn't say anything. Most don't when my praise can't be contained and overflows my lips . . .

Later that day, hours after my appointment, John 16:33 came to mind. The whole verse, not just the part from my morning devotions. "In the world you will have tribulation, but," as the Living Bible says, "cheer up for I have overcome the world." With this verse on my mind, I recalled my doctor's earlier question to me, "Do you ever get mad at life?" At that moment, thanks sprang up in my heart. Thanks because God had reminded me during my morning devotions of His truth through John 16:33. Later, when my doctor's question came, I had that truth right on the tip of my tongue, ready to be spoken. "We're told that we'll suffer—have trials." At that moment, joy welled up inside me. For you see, I love planting seeds of truth in a world of half-truths and lies.

Peace and the Needle Biopsy

You surround me with songs of victory. (Psalm 32:7b)

Three days before my scheduled needle biopsy, I read Mark 6:50 during my morning devotions. "It's all right," he said. "It is I! Don't be afraid." I also read Mark 6:56, "and as many as touched Him were healed." That night, I read some passages from Deuteronomy 7 and Deuteronomy 31. Both of those passages spoke of not being afraid as well. God's "do not be afraid" messages to me continued.

With God's help, I was not afraid, until that is, I was on my way out the door for my needle biopsy. A wave of fear came crashing over me then, so I went back to my bedroom and got my Bible. I opened it quickly and found that I had opened it to the book of Psalms. Psalm 32:7b was the verse my eyes fell upon. "You surround me with songs of *victory*" (emphasis mine). That was all I needed to read. Peace regained, I closed my Bible and hurried to the car.

God's peace remained with me throughout the whole procedure. The biopsy was not painful and the doctor, along with his assistants and myself, were talking during the procedure . . . even laughing. When the doctor found out my medical history, he said, "It's a miracle you're here." He also told me as he looked at the abnormality in my breast, "This is nothing. But we'll send it to the lab just to be sure." I considered that maybe "victory" was close at hand.

After the biopsy, Pete, Zach and I went to my sister-in-law and brother-in-law's home for a family Christmas party, and we had a great time that evening. Christmas was only three days away.

I was told I would get the results of the biopsy after Christmas. With the unknown surrounding me, I knew two things were certain. Number one: Satan would try to steal my joy that Christmas 2000, and number two: With God's help, I wouldn't let him!

Fish, Loaves and Hope

The disciples replied, "And where would we get enough here in the desert for all this mob to eat?" Jesus asked them, "How much food do you have?" And they replied, "Seven loaves of bread and a few small fish!" (Matthew 15:33–34)

Christmas Eve was two days after my biopsy. On that day, Pete, Zach and I went to a late afternoon Christmas service at church, followed by dinner at home. After a yummy dinner and fun conversation, we opened gifts. Zach was thirteen years old that Christmas, and it was the first year that he had bought our gifts with his own hard-earned money. One of the gifts I opened that night from Zach was a little resin church that held a pack of Bible verses. The displayed verse was Psalm 9:10, "Those who know your name will trust in you, for you, Lord, have never forsaken those who seek you" (NIV). God was speaking. No, He would not forsake me, not ever! My focus remained heavenward.

The day after Christmas, I got a call from my gynecologist that I was okay. It was, in his words, "the best Christmas present," but he didn't go into any specifics. "Victory" had come! I had known that it would, I just hadn't known when. The following day, though, I got another message on the answering machine from my gynecologist saying I needed to call him at his office the next day. Why in the world did I need to call him? I wondered.

When I woke up the next morning, I read my devotions before calling him. I didn't understand one of the verses, so I got out my Bible with study notes in it. When turning to that verse in question, I happened to open to Matthew 15, which contains the story of Jesus' miracle with the fishes and loaves. It was bookmarked. On the right-hand page, I noticed I had underlined something in the study notes at an earlier time. I stopped then to read it again. It mentioned the fact that God will care for us like He has in the past but that we, like the disciples, often forget that fact. It also urged the reader, when faced with a difficult situation to remember God's care for them in the past and to trust Him to be faithful again. After reading that, I cringed. I was just about to call my gynecologist back . . .

I went to the phone and dialed his number. When he got on the phone, he told me that I had breast cancer—cancer number four! His earlier good news was regarding my blood work, *not* the biopsy. The next step would be a lumpectomy. "Victory" hadn't arrived yet . . .

After getting the news, I went and reread the Bible notes. I was amazed that God had supplied them just prior to my conversation with the gynecologist. Through those Bible notes, God reminded me that He had cared for me time and time again. Yes, He would work faithfully on my behalf again. My part would be to trust him . . . again.

I called another dear sister-in-Christ, Deb Johnson, and shared the news with her. I also read the study notes to her. After our conversation, I opened the Bible again to reread those notes, only this time, I read all the study notes for the passage, not just the underlined part. The rest of the notes went on to say that even though the disciples had already seen Jesus feed more than five thousand people with five loaves and two fish, in a similar situation, they were perplexed. The notes also mentioned that we easily throw up our hands in despair when faced with difficult circumstances. The next words were the underlined ones, the ones I had read before talking to the gynecologist. I was excited. GOD WAS SPEAKING! He was reminding me then to remember all that He had done for me already—all the miracles of the past.

Later that day, I read a story from a book I had received for Christmas from Pete. It was a collection of short stories, and I had been reading one story a day after receiving it. The story for that day referred to Jesus' fish and loaves miracle!

The following day, I met with the surgeon who would do the lumpectomy. When I woke up that morning, a song was blasting in my mind. It was the same song that the kids' choir had sung at church a couple weeks prior that spoke of "my deliverer" coming and standing by. It gave me great comfort and strength on the way to my appointment with the surgeon.

That afternoon, after meeting with the surgeon, I picked up a book I was rereading, although it had been awhile since I had last picked it up. Chapter seven, the place where I had left off, was the story of the fish and loaves miracle! I sensed another miracle was in the making.

Two days later, on a Sunday, I decided to start reading another book I had received for Christmas. It was a fictional book that supposedly was very captivating. I was on page seven when I read, "(She) dreamt of the Lord feeding the five thousand on a hillside . . ."

That night, my dear neighbor and sister-in-Christ, Liz, stopped by with a gift for me. It was a sign that said, "Expect a miracle." God was working, I then believed, another miracle. YES! "Victory" *was* on the way. On the way . . .

Answered Prayer

I call on you, O God, for you will answer me.
(Psalm 17:6, NIV)

The day before my lumpectomy, I read my daily flip calendar. It mentioned the fact that nothing can touch us apart from God's will. It also stated that God will never fail us or forsake us and that the purpose of everything that happens to us is to build us up. Yes, God had allowed my situation, I told myself, and through it He would build me up and would never leave me. I also read Psalm 24:8, "The Lord, strong and mighty, invincible in battle!" Although I was weak, *He* was strong, invincible. The battle was in His hands, so was the victory. All I needed to do was trust. Those were tremendously encouraging words from God the day before surgery, and I was filled with His peace and His strength.

That night in bed, before I went to sleep, I read Psalm 108. Verse six stood out for me. "Hear the cry of your beloved child—come with mighty power and rescue me." Those words became my prayer that night. Psalm 107:29 also stood out for me, "He calms the storm and stills the waves." Those were more encouraging words from God. After reading them, I pictured Jesus stilling the waves of the storm around me. It was a powerful picture to fall asleep to just hours before surgery.

The next morning before Pete and I left, I happened to read Deuteronomy 31:6, "Be strong! Be courageous! Do not be afraid . . . " I said those words to myself over and over again, and also to Zach. It was a great verse for the day ahead. I also reminded Zach that he could talk to Jesus any time that day if he got scared. I then prayed for the Lord to surround me with Christians at the hospital.

After Pete and I arrived at the Breast Center connected with the hospital, Papa Don, (my friend Deb's dad) showed up, the first Christian God sent my way that day. Through Papa Don, I felt God's presence and love. We talked for a while before the nurse called my name. Papa Don stayed with Pete.

A needle was inserted into my breast before surgery as a guide for the surgeon. With the needle inserted, I needed a mammogram to make sure the needle was in the right location. While the technician did the mammogram, I happened to notice her bracelet. It had the letters WWJD on it, letters which, as a Christian, I knew stood for the question, "What would Jesus do?" I touched her bracelet and told her about my prayer that morning—that the Lord would surround me with Christians. She smiled. I smiled. She was the second Christian God sent me that day.

After the mammogram I was taken, along with Pete and Papa Don, to the hospital where the lumpectomy would be done. When we arrived, our visitation pastor from church was there to see us—the third Christian to arrive on the scene. After the nurse talked to me alone, the others joined me in the room where I waited to be called for surgery, and we prayed. Covered in prayer by the time the nurse came back, I was ready for surgery.

I was told the surgery would take about an hour, but in fact, it only took thirty-five minutes. When it was over, I was brought to the recovery room.

In the recovery room, someone said, "Hi", and I sensed she knew me by the way she said it. I couldn't see who it was, though, until she gave me my glasses. The "mystery" person was a woman from our church, a fellow greeter from our Tuesday morning Bible study—Christian number four.

I told her my earlier prayer, just like I had told the technician who had done the mammogram. After she heard about my prayer, she went to get another volunteer, Christian number five, and he told me that a lot of the nurses in the recovery room were Christians. I was truly surrounded!

In answer to prayer, I was definitely surrounded by Christians the day of my lumpectomy. I was thankful that the Lord had opened my eyes to recognize some of them. In so doing, He had made His own wonderful presence known to me. And even though I knew that day that He was with me, I was blessed by the tangible evidence of His presence and love. It was a blessing that continued to encourage me as I awaited the results of the lumpectomy.

A Promise to Rebuild

I will build you up again and you will be rebuilt.
(Jeremiah 31:4, NIV)

After my lumpectomy, I was told to call the surgeon's office four days later to get the lab results. On that day, I read my morning devotions, which stated five times that the Lord will not forsake us. I also read from a book Zach had given me for Christmas, wherein Hebrews 13:5 appeared, "For He has said, 'I will never leave you or forsake you'" (NRSV).

Although I fully believed God's word to me that I would have "victory" (i.e. be healed again), that particular morning I began to sense that the "victory" might come at a later time.

With those "delayed victory" thoughts on my mind, I wasn't looking forward to calling the surgeon's office. Was radiation or chemotherapy in the near future? I wondered . . .

For lunch that day, I went out with my dear-sister-in Christ, Jill. After Jill and I finished eating, another dear-sister-in Christ, Deb, joined us. Then the three of us went to my house to make the call to the surgeon's office.

Back at home, I really didn't want to make the call, but I knew that I had to. So with my sisters-in-Christ surrounding me, I picked up the phone and dialed the number. I was told they would have to get back to me. Unable to do anything more, I hung up the phone and we waited . . . Then we waited some more . . . Still no call.

Eventually, Deb had to go to work, and she told me to call the office one more time before she left. During that second call to the surgeon's office, I was told that the pathology wouldn't be available for another hour or so but that they would call me when they received the report. I hung up the phone again, and shared the news with Deb and Jill.

Finally, Deb had to leave. After she left, Jill and I went back to Coffee Creek (the coffee shop where we had had lunch) to get a treat. A short time later, I left to pick up Zach from school. Before I left, though, Jill told me she'd meet us back at our place in about half an hour.

As we pulled into the driveway, I asked Zach to get the mail for me. In the pile of mail was a card from Joan, another dear sister-in-Christ from our Bible study at church.

Inside the house, I checked the answering machine, and there was a message from Deb's dad, Papa Don. Before I called him back, I opened the card from Joan. In her card, she told me that the morning she had written the card, she was reading Jeremiah 31 and that verses three and four had stood out to her in her morning devotions. She also told me that she was claiming those verses for me. I quickly grabbed my Bible and opened to Jeremiah. I turned to chapter 31:3–4 and read, "The Lord appeared to us in the past, saying: "I have loved you with an everlasting love; I have drawn you with loving-kindness. I will build you up again and you will be rebuilt, O Virgin Israel. Again you will take up your tambourines and go out to dance with the joyful"(NIV). Immediately, I felt strengthened and encouraged by Joan's words to me . . . God's words to me.

While I pondered those words some more, Jill showed up, and I grabbed the phone to call Papa Don back. Phone in hand, I looked out the window and noticed someone pulling into our driveway. Papa Don! He had stopped by to see how I was doing, and after chatting for a while, I picked up the phone to call the surgeon's office again. I still hadn't heard back from them.

During that third call, I was told that the surgeon had seen only part of my lab report, and he needed to see the full report before he talked to me. I was told he'd call me the next morning. Waiting was nothing new for us . . .

Amazingly, at almost five o'clock that night, the surgeon himself called me back. Jill was gone by then, but Papa Don was at my side. The surgeon said he had "Good news/bad news for me." He explained that they hadn't found cancer in any of the surrounding tissue, but that he couldn't rule out cancer in other parts of the breast. The next step would be to meet with an oncologist. I asked him what he thought the recommended treatment would be and he said, "Most likely a double mastectomy." After hanging up with him, I was sad, but not defeated. For God had spoken to me, and I knew the surgeon's news couldn't change God's promise of "victory" for me.

Pete arrived shortly after I heard from the surgeon, and I immediately shared the sad news with him. Soon after that, Papa Don told us that he had to meet his wife Gail. They were meeting at a restaurant right up the road, and he invited us to join them. We said we'd talk about it and then said goodbye.

After Papa Don left, I called Deb and Jill with the news and cried. During my conversation with Deb, she encouraged me to go out to dinner with her parents. After our phone call I discussed it with Pete and Zach, and together we decided to join them.

Joan's verses to me from Jeremiah stayed with me that evening. As the evening wore on, we even laughed about God's choice of words to me from Jeremiah. We wondered what the "rebuilt" me would look like—"The 2001 model!" For I was flatter than a pancake . . .

Later in bed, I questioned God in prayer. Had the, "victory" message been for the biopsy only?

The next morning in my devotional book, God again spoke "victory." This time through 1 Corinthians 15:57: "But thanks be to God, who gives us the *victory* through our Lord Jesus Christ" (NRSV, emphasis mine).

I *would be* rebuilt—victory would come. But like I had also read during that time, "there are no victories without battles."

For My Good

He gives you grace to count the hardest spot the sweetest place. (J. Danson Smith)

The week before my double mastectomy surgery, I felt a strong urging to finish writing endings for a few stories I had written months before. So one day, I found the stories and selected one to work on.

The one I chose was a story about God's grace (see Radiation and the Nurse), how God's grace is sufficient and how it will always see us through. I was ready to write the ending, and I prayed for God's help. But as I sat there with pen in hand, nothing came to me. Nothing at all. Eventually, I put the story away. I just wasn't feeling inspired. Before I went to bed that night, I prayed again that God would help me to write that ending.

The next morning when I woke up, I read my devotions, and tucked within them was a poem.

And for my good this thing must be,
His grace sufficient for each test.
So still I'll sing whatever be
God's way for me is always best.

I finished reading that poem and knew that it was the answer to my prayer the night before!—the prayer for an ending to my story on grace. Thanks and praise filled my heart. I read it over and over again. I then marveled at God's amazing ways while I listed them individually in my mind . . .

1. The week before my double mastectomy, God had filled me with an urge to finish writing some stories I had written months before—even though I had plenty of other things to do before my surgery.

2. God somehow placed the story on Grace in my hands when there were others to choose from in the pile.

3. God supplied the ending for the story the next day in answer to my prayer the previous night.

4. God used that poem just days before surgery to encourage me, instruct me, and also to remind me that His grace is sufficient.

As I considered God's amazing ways that day, Esther's story in the Bible came to mind. Although God is never directly mentioned in Esther's story, there's no doubt regarding His presence and amazing ways in her life. I then realized anew that in my life, too, there's no doubt of His presence and amazing ways ...

Rescued From Danger

I cannot count the times when you have faithfully rescued me from danger. (Psalm 71:15a)

Following the surgeon's orders, after getting my lumpectomy results, I met with my oncologist. She, too, believed that a double mastectomy would be the best course of action. So after more doctor visits, lab work, shots to raise my white count and phone calls, a surgery date was set for my double mastectomy.

The days prior to my surgery, I was filled with a deep sense of peace. I was covered in the prayers of God's people, and I could tangibly feel those prayers. I believed with all my heart that victory was on the way ... for God had spoken it.

After getting into bed the night before surgery, though, I was overcome by fear. The battle raged for twenty minutes until I started repeating memorized Bible verses over and over to myself and got my focus back on the Lord. Peace then returned, and I slept soundly.

It was a short night's sleep, though, because Pete and I had to check in at the hospital at 5:30 A.M. prior to surgery. Papa Don unexpectedly joined us bright and early at the hospital, and I was so thankful he was there. Like Barnabas was to Paul, Papa Don was there to encourage me step by step.

After a short visit with Papa Don, I was whisked away by a nurse. Before I left, though, Papa Don asked me how my fear level was the night before. I told him then about the twenty-minute battle with fear and the ultimate "peace" victory. Thankfully, peace still reigned in my heart.

During my surgery, friends from my Bible study group, sisters-in-Christ, gathered in the hospital chapel to pray. Knowing that they were there strengthened me beyond words, and I was so very thankful.

My surgery, which also included part one of breast reconstruction, took about half the scheduled time. God answered those prayers from the chapel and from others.

My hospital stay went well, and I kept free of infection. I was told I had to sleep on my back for two weeks, which I thought would be impossible, but I was able to because God answered our prayers.

Home from the hospital, I was tired and weak, but every day I felt carried by the Lord, covered in prayer. Day by day, God strengthened me and encouraged me through His Word, through others, through cards, books and music.

Almost two weeks after surgery, I received great news from my surgeon—no cancer was found in any of the remaining right breast tissue or the lymph nodes that were removed. Praise and thanks overflowed my heart, touching heaven above.

Just before I received the great news from my surgeon, I had read Psalm 71 during my morning devotions. Verses 14 through 16 had stood out to me. After the call, I reread them. "I will keep on expecting you to help me. I praise you more and more. I cannot count the times when you have faithfully rescued me from danger. I will tell everyone how good you are, and of your constant, daily care. I walk in strength of the Lord God. I tell everyone that you alone are just and good."

How fitting I would read Psalm 71 that day. It perfectly described my situation—my life. God had once again, as the Psalm says, "faithfully rescued me from danger." Victory had come, bringing with it more stories to tell of how good God is and of His constant, daily care. I could sing of His love forever. I could sing of His love forever.

A Visit and a Reminder

How precious it is, Lord, to realize that you are
thinking about me constantly! (Psalm 139:17)

The weekend I got home from the hospital following my double mastectomy, I was more than anxious to wash my dirty hair. I had decided to wash it downstairs in our basement sink and I told Pete my plan. After listening, Pete got an idea. He told me that he could get a hose attachment for the downstairs faucet with a shower on it. I didn't really think that the attachment was necessary. Pete, though, pleased with his idea, headed out to the hardware store to buy one. He returned shortly and had the attachment hooked up and ready to go in no time at all. Pete and I headed downstairs to try it out.

Downstairs I gingerly undressed because I still had drain tubes inserted from my double mastectomy surgery and didn't want to catch the tubes on anything. The thought of accidentally pulling one of them out sent shivers down my spine.

Ready to wash my hair, I stood at the sink with Pete at my side. I got my hair wet and applied shampoo. Then Pete, holding the new shower attachment, turned the water on right over my head, to rinse . . . but it was more than a little rinse! The water seemed to be going everywhere! I got drenched and started crying. I yelled at Pete to turn the water off! The faucet attachment hadn't been a good idea after all. Pete felt horrible. I was frustrated, shook up and sopping wet.

From upstairs, Zach heard all the commotion and joined us in the basement. He also felt bad for me and offered to help. After getting the shampoo out, I dried my hair, put on my dry clothes and went upstairs to our living room. Still upset, I sat down and tried to relax. As I sat there alone, I thought to myself, *These are the times when I wish Mom was still living!*

My thoughts were interrupted by my dear sister-in-Christ, Kary, who had arrived bearing bright balloons and gifts. When Kary saw me, she smiled, joined me on the couch and gave me a big hug. I told her what had just happened and she stayed to chat for a while.

During our conversation, Kary shared some of her feelings about being a mom and wife. She seemed to be in need of encouragement that day, too.

As I thought about Kary's words, I remembered something. That morning, I had reread parts of a book I had read a long time ago. I had recently pulled the book out to look for a poem or story to share with friends for Valentine's Day. I had found two possible choices—one a poem, the other a story. As Kary and I talked, I realized that the story I had found was meant for her encouragement that day. I opened the book and read it to her.

Kary stayed a while longer before heading out. Her visit was like a kiss from above. I knew that God had sent her . . . in His perfect timing.

After Kary left, Pete joined me in the living room, and by that time, we both laughed as we recalled the earlier hair-washing escapade.

Later on, I considered how God had known our needs (Kary's and mine) by encouraging both of us that morning. He encouraged me through Kary's perfectly timed visit; Kary, by a story He had caused me to recall. Psalm 139:2, 17–18 says, "You know when I sit or stand. When far away you know my every thought. How precious it is, Lord, to realize that you are thinking about me constantly! I can't even count how many times a day your thoughts turn towards me. And when I waken in the morning, you are still thinking of me!"

How comforting it is to know that God is thinking about me constantly . . . that He knows when I sit or stand, or even when I'm getting drenched, washing my hair.

At times I forget that truth, but when I do, God lovingly reminds me. Sometimes He reminds me through His Word, other times through a card, a phone call or even a visit by a friend at just the right time—like Kary's visit that day.

Thank you, Lord, for reminding me that you are constantly thinking about me. Thank you, Kary, for being His messenger that day ...

P.S. The day I finished writing this story, I was feeling awful. I hadn't been feeling well for several days, but on that day I was feeling especially awful. After months of dealing with medical issues, I was also feeling somewhat discouraged (something I rarely feel because of my great hope in Jesus Christ). After I finished writing that day, I saw someone pull into our driveway. Who was it? Kary!! Another perfectly timed visit—another reminder from above. "How precious it is, Lord, to realize that you are thinking of me constantly!" (Psalm 139:17). Thank you, Lord. Thank you, Lord ...

A poem I wrote especially for my Bible Study group– January 2001

How can I thank you for all of your prayers,
For all of the wonderful ways that you care?

How can I thank you, what shall I do
To show you how thankful I am for you?

Shall I buy you a gift?
Oh, what could it be?
To show you how much you mean to me?

Shall I write you a song,
To keep in your heart?
A song to remember when we are apart?

Shall I make you a gift
And wrap it with love?
A gift that's inspired by heaven above?

No, I shall not buy you a gift,
Write a song,
Or make you a gift to take along.

But rather I'll ask our Father above
To bless you and keep you,
Each day with His love.

To reveal His purposes,
His plans for you.
To guide you each day,
Your whole life through.

To grant you His strength,
His joy, His peace.
To carry your burdens,
To grant you relief.

To shine through your life
Wherever you are . . .
To the lost and confused
Both near and far.

To fill you with thanks
And songs of praise
No matter what circumstances
Mark your days.

And before I close
I will thank Him again
For bringing YOU
Into my life, dear friend.

The Scheduler, The Insurance Company and God's Spirit

'Not by might nor by power, but by my Spirit,'
says the Lord Almighty. (Zechariah 4:6, NIV)

After meeting with my oncologist, who informed me that I indeed had to undergo a double mastectomy, I was scheduled for an appointment with a surgeon, the same surgeon who performed my lumpectomy.

The day of my appointment with him, I read my devotions. Psalm 46:5 stood out to me, "He will not delay His help." I was thankful for such encouraging words to carry in my heart on the way to my appointment that morning.

At the appointment, my surgeon talked a little more about my upcoming double mastectomy, and he answered questions that Pete and I had for him. When our meeting with the surgeon was over, he brought us to the woman in his office who schedules surgeries for him.

After looking over some paperwork, the scheduler told us that she still needed to get approvals and referrals from the insurance company before we could get a date on the calendar for my surgery. I asked her how long that would take, and she said she had no idea. She told us that it was very difficult to get the right people on the phone. She also said the insurance company had to approve taking my right breast, since cancer was only found in the left. Sitting in her office, I couldn't believe what I was hearing! It was cancer #4 we were talking about here! Wasn't there any urgency in getting the surgery done?!

Before leaving her office, Pete and I asked if there was anything *we* could do to speed up the process. She said no. We left her office not knowing when in the world we would hear back from her or when in the world my double mastectomy would be.

Back home, I got down on my knees and prayed that God would work it out, that He would put it heavy on the scheduler's heart to work on my case and that she would be able to get the right people on the phone, including the doctors. I decided then to walk by faith, not by sight.

Around lunchtime, I got a call from a dear sister-in-Christ. After she heard about our dilemma, she told me to call the scheduler back and in her words, "dig your heels in." She also suggested that I tell them that if my diagnosis was different because "they took their time," they would be hearing from us! After talking to her, though, I didn't feel God putting that on my heart to do. Instead, I felt peace, knowing God was in control.

Around three o'clock that same day, an idea came to me. I could simply call the scheduler back and ask her if she had made any progress with contacting doctors, the insurance company, and so on. It seemed like a good idea, so I picked up the phone and called her. The scheduler told me right away that everything was taken care of, and she proceeded to give me my surgery date!

After that phone call, Zechariah 4:6 came to me, "'Not by might nor by power, but by my Spirit,' says the Lord Almighty" (NIV). I praised God over and over for working it out by His Spirit—His Spirit alone.

That night in bed, I remembered the verse that had stood out to me that morning: "He will not delay His help" (Psalm 46:5). God certainly had not delayed His help that day, and thanks and praise once again filled my heart.

That evening I also read this, "And the moment their faith began to work, the blessing came." The moment I chose to walk by faith that day, the blessings came. God filled me with His peace, then later, He opened my eyes so that I could recognize His Holy Spirit's power in solving my dilemma— just hours after praying.

Walk by faith or walk by sight? It's a choice I face every single day on the journey of life. To walk by faith isn't always easy but, with God's help, it's always possible. And I wondered to myself then what blessings I have missed when I have chosen instead to walk by sight.

Sally's Devotional Book?

But thanks be to God, who gives us the victory through our Lord Jesus Christ. (1 Corinthians 15:57, NRSV)

Pete, Zach and I were at a local Christian bookstore one night, just weeks before my breast cancer diagnosis. Zach and Pete were listening to CDs while I looked for a new devotional book. Standing in front of the devotional section, I prayed that God would lead me to the devotional He had in mind for me at that time. It was a prayer I had never prayed before.

After looking at a few books, I felt drawn to one in particular. A short time later, we purchased that book and drove home.

At home and in bed, I picked up the newly purchased devotional and read through several devotions before falling asleep that night. As I read, I questioned why God had directed me to that particular devotional. The devotions seemed to be for someone going through a major trial, which at the time I wasn't. While contemplating that fact, I remembered a woman I had recently met named Sally. Sally had breast cancer and was going through a hard time. *Maybe the devotional was for her*, I thought to myself. I was going to see Sally at a Christmas event the following week, and after giving it more thought the next day I decided to give the devotional to her.

The following week arrived, and I headed to the Christmas event, devotional in hand. At the event, I learned that Sally couldn't make it that evening because she wasn't feeling well. I planned then to give it to her at another time.

The next week, I called Sally. I told her that I had something for her and that if it were okay, I would drop it off at her home that evening. She told me that the traffic was bad at that time and that I should just bring it at a later date. Even though I didn't mind the traffic, I sensed that it just wasn't a good time for Sally. I decided to call Sally back later.

That was early December, and soon after I was busy with Christmas decorating, shopping and more. This was the same time I found out that I needed a second mammogram. After that second mammogram, a needle biopsy was ordered. The biopsy was done a couple of days before Christmas. I tried calling Sally again but she wasn't available. The devotional remained with me.

The last week in December, I found out that I did indeed have breast cancer, and a lumpectomy was scheduled for the first week in January. By that time, I had forgotten about my plan of giving the devotional to Sally.

During that time God's repeated message to me was "victory." It seemed that one word kept popping up everywhere I turned. I had the lumpectomy on January 4th, and two days later, I was paging through a book I had received for Christmas. One paragraph in particular stood out to me. It spoke of the bruising and bumps we go through when God sends us places. It also mentioned how God tests our faith through the bumps He allows to see if we will believe what he has spoken to us no matter what. *He had said victory*, I thought to myself. And I was determined to stick with what God had promised me. When I opened my Bible that night, my eyes landed on Psalm 32:7b "You surround me with songs of victory." (The same verse I had read the day of my needle biopsy.)

A couple nights later, I questioned the Lord. Was the victory for the biopsy only? His answer came the next morning when in one of my devotionals I read 1 Corinthians 15:57: "But thanks be to God, who gives us the victory through our Lord Jesus Christ" (NRSV). I knew that I would survive whatever lay ahead.

The day after reading 1 Corinthians 15:57, I remembered the devotional I had bought, the one I had purchased for myself but had planned to give to Sally. I unwrapped "Sally's" devotional that day and started reading it again. By that time it was January 10, 2001, and after reading for a while, I realized that God had definitely directed me to the right devotional that night at the bookstore. He knew the trial I would be undergoing. It was for me after all.

The next day, I decided to go back and read all the December readings from the devotional. I wanted to know what messages from God I had missed! I turned to December 1, the day I had purchased the book, and could hardly believe what I read: "Thanks be to God! He gives us the victory through our Lord Jesus Christ." 1 Corinthians 15:57, again! Victory . . . again! From that day forward, I read that devotional book every day. And every day, I was anxious to see what God had to say to me through the daily scriptures, stories and poems. God mightily used that book during my breast cancer. It was the perfect devotional for me, and God had known that it would be. That's why He had directed me to it when I stood in front of the devotional section at the store that night. That's also why I had been prevented from giving it to Sally.

Looking back, I realize that God wanted to prepare me and encourage me through the words of that devotional starting back on December 1. He wanted me to hear the "victory" message from day one. But since His directions in buying that book didn't make sense to me at the time, I had planned on giving the book to Sally.

Remembering the night I purchased the devotional, I realized that more times than not, God's directions to me don't make sense. At those times, though, I must remember that He is God and that He knows the future. Like Isaiah 55:9 says, "For just as the heavens are higher than the earth, so are my ways higher than yours, and my thoughts than yours."

Next time, may I fully trust God no matter what the written words on the page may say, just as in the case of that "God-directed" devotional. And may I also trust Him fully, even when the words on the page of my life don't make sense to me. For He knows my story from beginning to end, my past and future experiences and each page along the way . . .

P.S. A couple days after reading the December devotions I had missed, I decided to go through some papers I had pulled out of our wicker chest the week before. Once I finished sorting, I still had energy left and I decided to take everything out of the wicker chest, vacuum it, and reorganize it. When I did, I came across an old brochure from the church my mom had attended years ago in Blue Earth, Minnesota. I had sorted through her things when my dad had passed away a couple years before then. But for some reason, I had kept the church brochure aside. I had planned to read it some day. I stopped sorting, picked it up and opened the cover. On the first page of that brochure, I read, "But thanks be to God who gives us the victory through our Lord Jesus Christ." 1 Corinthians 15:57 . . . again!

The Valentine Gifts

So I say, live by the Spirit. (Galatians 5:16, NIV)

Valentine's Day 2001 was one week after my double mastectomy surgery. I was recovering at home, and that afternoon my dear sister-in-Christ, Carolynn, stopped by with some Valentine treats.

Zach was already home from school, and as Carolynn and I talked, I heard him go into his room and shut the door behind him. He was in his room for a long time, and during my visit with Carolynn, I wondered what in the world he was doing.

About an hour later, Zach emerged from his room and joined Carolynn and me in the living room. In his hands were handmade Valentine gifts. That's what he had been busy doing in his room! I was practically speechless as he presented them to me.

The first gift he gave me was an adorable vase with flowers. The vase and flowers were all made out of paper and then decorated with markers. The vase actually stood up, and the flowers had stems made out of rolled-up paper. I was over-whelmed by his creativity and kindness. The second gift from Zach was a heart cutout that was decorated with a pencil design, markers and candy hearts. The third gift he made for me was a handmade decorated envelope on which was written, "The Love Seeds." While I examined it, Zach told me that inside were little pieces of paper with letters written on them. He instructed me then to pick one, which I did. He then told me to pick one letter a day until they were all gone. After that I was to figure out a hidden message using those letters.

As the days went by, I was anxious to know that hidden message, and some days Zach let me draw more than one letter from the "Love Seeds" envelope.

Five days later, I picked the last letter! With Zach at my side, I spread the letters out on our living room ottoman, ready to solve the mystery. As I worked on it, Zach offered one little clue, and in no time at all I figured it out. Zach's hidden message to me was, "Victory, the best is yet to come." From the mouths of babes . . .

The day before and even that morning, I had felt my enemy, discouragement, trying to ambush me. God knew that I was in need of encouragement. He also knew that encouragement was on the way. For Zach was His messenger and five days earlier on Valentine's Day, He had given Zach the message He knew I would need. Tears came to my eyes as I relayed to Zach how God had used him to remind me of the "victory" God had already promised me.

The same day I figured out Zach's hidden message, I took the individual letters and glued them on a piece of paper. I then placed that piece of paper on our antique pump organ where I was sure to spot it each day. God continued to use that message throughout my recovery to encourage and brighten my days.

After originally solving the hidden message, I asked Zach how he had come up with the idea for the Valentine gifts and the message itself. He said he didn't know, but later God reminded me of this: everyday before Zach goes to school, we pray together. One of my prayers during that prayer time is always the same—that God would guide our thoughts, words and deeds that day by His Holy Spirit. Galatians 5:16 says "So I say, live by the Spirit, and you will not gratify the desires of the sinful nature" (NIV). God revealed to me that Zach's actions that Valentine's Day were an answer to our daily prayer. Zach had been led by the Holy Spirit.

What a privilege it was to witness the Spirit at work in Zach's life through those Valentine gifts he made for me. Much of Zach's days are spent in school, and I don't always get that privilege. I do trust that there are signs of the Spirit displayed in his life there, too—maybe through a kind word, a kind deed or more.

After witnessing the Spirit at work in Zach's life, I was encouraged to continue praying that daily prayer with him. I was also reassured that, yes, it's true—teenagers *can* be led by the Spirit, not just the flesh. And I now have tangible evidence of that fact: a solved message and an empty "Love Seeds" envelope.

Tea, a Belated Gift and More

Call to me and I will answer you. (Jeremiah 33:3, NIV)

One day, a couple months after my double mastectomy, I got a call from my dear friend and sister-in-Christ, Nannette. She called to invite me over for tea and to give me a present, a belated present from when I was in the hospital. She had planned to stop by our place weeks earlier to give me that present, but twice she had run into Jeanne, another dear sister-in-Christ, who had told her to give me more time to get my strength back before visiting.

Finally, I was stronger, and Nannette invited me over. When I got to her house the day of our visit, she had water on the stove for tea. Shortly after I arrived, she invited me into her dining room, and we sat down at her dining room table. For some reason, in our conversation that afternoon, Nannette mentioned *Guidepost* magazine and the fact that she subscribed to it. Right at that moment I remembered an article I had been searching for, and I told her about it. She then told me that she had lots of back issues and that maybe she had the one I was looking for. She got up from the table to take a quick look.

Nannette returned with several issues in her hands, but as we looked at the dates, we couldn't find any from 1997, the year I needed. Nannette told me then that I could take those issues home with me. Looking them over, though, I realized that I had already read most of them. For a while, I had gotten my dad's subscription for that magazine after he died in 1998. Looking over Nannette's issues, I did find three, though, that I hadn't read yet, and I put them by my purse so I'd remember to take them home with me.

That night in bed, I reached for the three magazines from Nannette. After looking at the covers, I decided to read the December 2000 issue. That issue featured a famous Christian artist on the cover. I was drawn to that particular issue because I had recently learned that a member from our church had opened a gallery featuring some of the artist's work. Before reading the article about that artist, however, I flipped to the back cover to look over the table of contents. I was surprised I didn't find a table of contents on the back like I had in past issues. There obviously had been a change in the magazine's layout.

I decided to open the back page anyway. I found two letters featured there, letters by readers that told about how previous stories from the magazine had changed their lives. I could hardly believe my eyes when I began reading the second letter—it was about the story I had been trying to find! It mentioned the name of the article and the exact date it had originally appeared. I had finally found it!

Within days, I received a copy of the article online from the magazine's customer service department. Later, I marveled as I considered the intricate details that had been woven together by God in my search for that article. Number 1: The fact that Jeanne had run into Nannette twice and told her to wait before visiting me. (Nannette and I probably wouldn't have talked about that magazine back then right after my surgery!) Number 2: The fact that Nannette had invited me to her place and that we had talked about that magazine during our visit. Number 3: The fact that Nannette had back issues of the magazine and gave me a few to take home with me. Number 4: The fact that I was drawn to the issue with the artist on the cover because I had recently heard at the time that someone from our church had opened a gallery featuring the artist.

Jeremiah 33:3 says, "Call to me and I will answer you" (NIV). The night I found the article's title and date in one of the back issues Nannette had given me, my heart rejoiced. God had heard my call for His help in finding the article and had sent it to me. Even though I had to wait on Him longer than I thought, I was blessed more than I could have imagined once the article was found. I was reminded anew of God's faithfulness when we call on Him in prayer, of His intricate plans woven into all of our lives and the fact that He works through the lives of His children each and every day. Sometimes when we don't even have a clue. Right, Jeanne? Right, Nannette?

"Spring to Life" Song

During my breast cancer, I planned a women's event with others at our church called "Spring to Life." At the time, God inspired me with this song for it:

You brought healing to my lost and wayward soul
You're the one who healed my body, made me whole
You saw my tears, heard my cries
Lord, you opened up my eyes
That I might see your face
That I might come to know your grace
Thank you, Lord, for my new life in You
Thank you, Lord, for my new life in You.

Breast Cancer—Summary/Lessons Learned

Almost two and a half years after my colon cancer diagnosis, I was diagnosed with breast cancer. A breast abnormality was detected on a routine mammogram, and I was called back for a second mammogram. Following a second mammogram, a needle biopsy was ordered to determine if the abnormality was cancerous or not. Days following the needle biopsy, I was called with the results. I was told that I did indeed have cancer once again, breast cancer . . . cancer number four.

For breast cancer, my treatment involved a double mastectomy and I chose to be rebuilt (to have breast reconstruction surgery)! I am now, like I once read elsewhere, "fearfully and artificially made" (instead of "fearfully and wonderfully made" as Psalm 139 describes)!

As in my previous cancers, God once again revealed Himself through His Word and others, that I would survive yet another bout with cancer, which I did. I praise God daily for His healing touch on my life, for His unbelievable mercy and for His amazing grace.

There were those around me who were angry with God for allowing another cancer to occur in my life. By God's grace, I was not angry with God. By His grace, I continued to keep my focus Heavenward, to fully trust Him with my future, to take Him at His revealed word to me (regardless of what others around me said), to praise Him and to thank Him. Through it all, God again supplied my every need, including filling me with His peace, His strength, His power, and His joy. Once again, He had unforgettable lessons for me to learn. Looking back, three specific lessons come to mind ...

1. I learned that God's joy is in those who expect Him to be loving and kind. Early on in my breast cancer journey, God drew my attention to Psalm 147: 11, "But His joy is in those who reverence Him, those who expect Him to be loving and kind." That verse stayed with me long after I read it. Although I felt that I already expected God to be loving and kind, after meditating on that verse, I began to more consciously expect His kindness and love. It was an amazing discovery for me, one that has stayed with me. I now try to live each day with an expectant heart. It is an exciting way to live this side of heaven. It not only brings joy to my Heavenly Father's heart but brings joy to my own as well.

2. I learned to thank God in advance for what He promised me through His Word. One day, while talking to my dear sister-in-Christ, Deb, I told her that God was speaking victory to me through various Bible verses and situations. She suggested to me then that I thank God in advance for His promised victory. After our conversation, Deb's words stayed with me. Although I had heard about thanking God in advance, I personally hadn't done that before. So I began to start thanking God in advance for His promised victory. It turned out to be another seed that God used to grow my faith, one that continues to bloom in the garden of my soul.

3. I learned to thank God for the opportunities trials present—opportunities to prove God's faithfulness to the world. One day during my quiet time with God, I found myself thanking Him for another opportunity to prove His faithfulness to the world around me through my breast cancer. After that prayer of thanksgiving, I stopped. I actually couldn't believe what I had just thanked God for. Was I crazy? But as I gave it more thought, it still seemed right. Although I couldn't actually say I was thankful for the cancer, I truly was thankful for the opportunities for witnessing to God's faithfulness that my breast cancer provided. Wow! I realized then how much God had grown my faith since my first bout with cancer. Afterwards, through several books and a song on the radio, God confirmed that, no, I wasn't crazy. He taught me that He is blessed and we are blessed when we can thank Him amidst trials—even for the trials themselves and the opportunities they present. In this world full of trials and

tribulations, I can choose to see trials as opportunities, opportunities to prove God's faithfulness to the world and to thank God for those opportunities.

Unbelievable as it is, I have survived cancer number four. Victory has come, just as God promised me. I stand in awe when I consider all the mighty things, all the miracles, that God has done for me. "He who is mighty has done great things for me and holy is His name" (Luke 1:49, NKJV). Because of God's great love and mercy, I am still alive today. And by His grace, I want to live my life so that each day is like a thank you note to Him for all that He has done.

Although I don't know what tomorrow may bring, I continue to live expectantly. Like an expectant child up on my tiptoes, I daily expect my Heavenly Father to be loving and kind. Writing about expecting things, I'm reminded of these words from one of my favorite songs:

I stand before the great eternal throne
The one that God Himself is seated on
And I, I've been invited as a son
Oh I, I've been invited to come and . . .

Chorus:
Believe the unbelievable
Receive the inconceivable
And see beyond my wildest imaginations
Lord, I come with great expectations.
(Steven Curtis Chapman)

With open hands and an open heart I come. I come. One day at a time. With great expectations . . .

Part Five
(God at Work in Ordinary Daily Life)

A Straight Path

I guide you in the way of wisdom and lead you along straight paths. (Proverbs 4:11, NIV)

My mind raced as Dad and I drove home from his doctor's appointment. During that appointment, Dad's doctor had gently and lovingly suggested that it was time for Dad to consider moving out of his house and into an assisted-living residence. Several weeks earlier, Dad had been diagnosed with liver cancer and was also suffering from memory loss. His doctor felt that an assisted-living residence would be the safest place for him to live.

My heart went out to Dad. The one who had so faithfully and lovingly cared for his family for so many years was now unable to live alone and care for himself. Dad had been so proud of the way he had taken care of the house and himself since Mom had died thirteen years prior. Cooking, laundry, housecleaning, yard work, grocery shopping and more—he had done it all.

Fiercely independent, Dad had rejected any of our earlier suggestions of a move. Riding home with me that day, though, he sat peacefully looking out the window. Who would have guessed that Dad would accept the idea of moving so quickly? So graciously? Not us, that's for sure. It seemed like a miracle to me, a miracle.

Shortly thereafter, we scheduled an appointment with a social worker to go over Dad's finances and to help us in our search for an assisted-living residence. My days were bathed in prayer as we began to look at the myriad of options. So many choices. So much to consider. From the start, I had asked God to guide us to the place that He had in mind for Dad. Every day, I anxiously anticipated a sign from above.

One day, I ran an errand with Zach. It was during rush hour and because the traffic was bad, I took an alternate route to our planned destination. At one point on that alternate route, we waited at a stoplight just down the road from our home. When the light changed, I took a left turn, and it was then that I spotted it—a small "Apartment Available" sign. The sign was hanging on a larger sign that said, "Elder Homestead." I had driven by Elder Homestead many times before, but their sign had never stood out to me like it did that particular day.

As I continued driving, I remembered something. Days earlier, my dear sister-in-Christ, Jeanne, had mentioned Elder Homestead as a possibility for Dad. At the time, we weren't sure just what kind of residence it was, though. Hmmm . . . It was when I had taken an alternate route that I had noticed the "Apartment Available" sign. I tucked that tidbit of information in my mind for safekeeping, and I knew that we had to at least check it out. My prayers for a clear sign from God grew more intense with each passing day.

I told Dad about the alternate route story and the "Apartment Available" sign. He agreed that we should check it out. The next week, we stopped by Elder Homestead to get some information. Upon leaving with brochures in hand, the woman we had talked to asked what my name was. "Tamara Windahl," I replied. "Tamara is my daughter's name," she answered. I walked to the car with Dad and thought about the fact that in my whole life I had only met a handful of others with the same name. Hmmm . . . another sign from God?

After looking through the brochures from Elder Homestead, Dad and I decided to set up a tour of the building and the available apartment. So I made a call, and a tour was arranged for the next day.

At Elder Homestead the following day, Dad and I were happy to find out that the available apartment was on a corner that received a lot of lovely sunshine. It was small but actually bigger than we had imagined. It had a separate bathroom and kitchen and also a common parlor outside the apartment for the four apartments in that section. From the start of the tour, it was obvious that Dad was sold on the place. I really liked it, too. We informed the woman who had given us the tour that we were very interested in the apartment. We also told her that we would give her a call within the next couple of days.

Leaving Elder Homestead after our tour that day, I drove by the front of the building. I mentioned to Dad that it reminded me of a Southern plantation because of the wrap-around porch.

On the way home, Dad was clearly excited and told me that Elder Homestead was where he wanted to live. I said I would be happy to take him to check out other places, too, but he said no. He truly thought that Elder Homestead was where he should move.

Since Elder Homestead was just down the road and left at the stoplight, we were home in no time at all. I made us lunch, during which time my mother-in-law called. She said that she was going to stop by to drop off my birthday present. I told her then where we had been, and she was anxious to hear the details. I gave her a little description of Elder Homestead and even mentioned the wrap-around porch which made it look like a Southern plantation.

After lunch and after my mother-in-law had dropped off my birthday present, I decided to rest for a while. I grabbed the new book I had gotten the day before for my birthday, anxious to begin reading it. I read the preface and turned to the first chapter. The first sentence of the chapter began by giving a year and then the setting: "from the wrap-around porch of his plantation-style home." It was then I knew for sure that God's plan for Dad was just down the road and left at the stoplight.

Proverbs 3:5–6 says, "Trust in the Lord with all your heart and lean not on your own understanding; in all your ways acknowledge Him, and He will make your paths straight" (NIV). I had acknowledged God, trusted Him, and He had directed us; He made Dad's "path straight." Through an "Apartment Available" sign, a name, a porch and a book . . .

When others questioned whether Elder Homestead was the right place for Dad because of his memory loss, Proverbs 3:5–6 repeatedly came to my mind. And I chose to trust God completely—not leaning on my own understanding or anyone else's. I chose to go God's way. For God had already taught me on my faith journey that His way is the best way ... always. Even when it doesn't make sense. Even when others don't understand.

Like breadcrumbs on a trail, God's signs led Dad home—to the perfect home for him just four months before he died. I am so thankful that God can be trusted. I am so thankful that He knows the way home ...

From the Hand of the Lord

Both riches and honor come from you. In your hand it is to make great and to give strength to all. Now, therefore, our God, we thank you and praise your glorious name. (1 Chronicles 29:12–13, NKJV)

Pete and I were all dressed up and on our way to his annual company party. During the car ride there, our conversation overflowed with excitement and anticipation. Before we arrived at the party, Pete reminded me of some of his fellow employee's names and the names of their spouses. This was something he always did before we arrived at the annual party each year. After the names ritual was over, we started talking about the possibility of Pete winning an employee award that night. As we talked, I asked him which award he would like to win if he had a choice. He told me the award, and I then asked him a simple question, never dreaming we would get into an argument over it. "If you do win an award, will you publicly give thanks to God?" Pete thought for a while before telling me that, no, he wouldn't—not at a work event. I was stunned. I couldn't believe what I was hearing. God had blessed us with so much and yet Pete wasn't willing to publicly give Him thanks? I had a sickening feeling inside after the words came out of his mouth. I was shocked. I was mad. I told him then that I was so sick of "closet" Christianity. "God should be a part of everything we do, and that includes work," I told him. He told me that I just didn't understand—that it was a different story at work.

We were still mad at each other when we got to the party, but we put it aside, not wanting to let the argument ruin our night out. At the party, we had a delicious dinner and a fun time catching up with those at our table. Following dinner was the awards presentation.

For each award, we were shown slides of the nominees before the winner was announced. When they got to the final award, I realized it was the award Pete had mentioned in the car, the one award he would like to win if he had a choice. For that final award, we were again shown slides of the nominees. Among those pictured was Pete! Would he actually win it after all?!

The winner was announced . . . Pete Windahl! Shocked and excited, we hugged each other as he got up from our table and proceeded to the podium to accept his award. I will never forget the first words out of his mouth that night. He began, "On the way here my wife asked me a question. She asked me if I did win an award, would I publicly give thanks to God?" He continued, "Yes, I'm going to do that."

Sitting in the audience I could hardly believe what I was hearing. While Pete spoke, his face beamed, my face beamed and everyone listened. God got the thanks, God got the glory and joy filled my heart.

1 Chronicles 29:12–13 says "Both riches and honor come from you. In your hand it is to make great and to give strength to all. Now, therefore, our God, we thank you and praise your glorious name" (NKJV). Pete's honor that night was from the hand of the Lord, and I was so glad that Pete was willing to step out in faith and publicly give thanks to God for it at his company party. That night, Pete chose to give credit where credit was due. And in so doing, hearts were touched and seeds were planted . . . spiritual seeds.

I have learned that there are many ways to plant spiritual seeds—bits of truth that point people to God, the Bible, or the Good News of Jesus Christ—in the hearts of the unbelieving world around me. And one of those ways is by publicly giving thanks to God for blessings we receive.

After Pete gave thanks to God at the company party, a few of his fellow employees came up to him and praised him for publicly thanking God. Like I said before, hearts were touched and seeds were planted. And I wouldn't be surprised if when we get to heaven one day, I hear someone say to Pete, "Remember when you gave thanks to God at our company party?" And we will then finally know the value of those seeds. Of those seeds.

Peace, Peace, Wonderful Peace

Now go ahead and do as I tell you, for I will
help you to speak well, and I will tell you what
to say. (Exodus 4:12)

Most every Sunday at our church, someone shares his/her faith story during the worship service—the story of how he/she came to a relationship with Jesus. After listening to many of those stories, I was amazed at how calm most of the people were as they spoke in front of our large congregation. *Not exactly how I'd be if I were up there!* I thought to myself. Personally, I dreaded public speaking. But God was at work, and things were about to change . . .

During announcements one Sunday, our pastor mentioned a card that was enclosed in the bulletin that morning. It was a card to fill out if you were interested in giving your faith story. Several months before that very moment in church, God had made it clear to me that someday I would give my faith story at church. Holding that card in my hand, I wondered if God's time had arrived. I honestly hoped that it hadn't because the thought of speaking in front of our congregation sent shivers down my spine. I quickly slipped the card back in the bulletin.

When Pete and I talked with our pastor following that service, he mentioned that he wanted me to put my faith story down on paper for him. My mind raced as our pastor's request sunk in. I was scared, but I agreed to do what he requested anyway.

The days following that conversation with our pastor, I prayed for God's help and began writing my faith story. God had revealed Himself so clearly to me during my cancer experiences and had been so faithful that, once I started writing, I wrote and I wrote and I wrote. When I finished writing, I folded up the finished faith story and put it in an envelope to deliver to our pastor.

With that project completed, I started sweeping our kitchen floor. As I swept, something occurred to me. The previous week, a Bible verse had played on my mind day after day. It was a verse from the story of Jesus and the woman at the well. "Many believed because of the woman's testimony." When that verse had stayed on my mind the week before, I had wondered why. The answer came when I was sweeping that day right after I finished writing my faith story. I realized then, after days of that verse playing on my mind, our pastor had asked me to write my faith story. "Many believed because of the woman's testimony." God was clearly at work. Through that verse He had been preparing me for what He was calling me to do—give my faith story at church; *my testimony*. The moment I realized God's confirmed plan for me, I was scared. I mean *scared*. Public speaking? Yikes!

After I delivered my faith story to our pastor the following Sunday, I got a call from our discipleship pastor, the one in charge of arranging the faith stories each month. He asked if I was willing to give my faith story some Sunday. I said, "Yes." Not because I wanted to, but because I sensed God calling me to do it.

After agreeing to give my faith story, I was told that there was an opening in the schedule for me either the first Sunday in July or else sometime in October. I was also told that most people had about six months to prepare their faith stories but that my story tied in especially well with the July sermon—only weeks away. He mentioned that Psalm 42 was the text for the July sermon. After I agreed to give my faith story in July, I hung up the phone, scared to death at the commitment I had made.

That night in bed, my mind raced. July was right around the corner. What was I thinking?! "But if that's when you want me to do it, Lord, that's when I'll do it," I prayed. After uttering that simple prayer, I remembered the Psalm 42 text that our pastor had mentioned during our conversation. I couldn't remember what Psalm 42 was about, and I knew that I wouldn't be able to sleep until I found out. So at eleven o'clock that night, I got out of bed, turned on the light and grabbed my Bible to look it up. "As the deer pants for water, so I long for you, O God" (Pslam 42:1). I stopped. I could hardly believe what I was reading . . .

Just the day before, I had been at my last piano lesson before summer vacation. At that lesson, my teacher, Joanne, had given me a copy of a song for me to try playing during the summer. It was a song I loved, and I had been singing it the day before. I had also been singing it that day just hours before looking up Psalm 42 in my Bible! The name of the song? "As the Deer"—a song based on Psalm 42!

I closed my Bible that night, convinced that the first Sunday in July was exactly the day God wanted me to give my faith story. His timing had arrived. He confirmed it through Psalm 42.

Back in bed and lying down again, I thought about how God knew about my fear of speaking in front of a crowd. I also thought about how He knew that I could never do it alone. With those thoughts on my mind, another thought came to me, a thought straight from heaven above. God would provide me with everything I needed to accomplish His will—the words He wanted me to say, His strength and His peace. Just like He had provided for Moses. With those comforting thoughts on my mind, I fell asleep. At peace and in the arms of my Heavenly Father.

Days later, I met with our discipleship pastor who helped me edit and fine-tune my faith story. After that meeting, I quickly got to the job at hand of rehearsing my faith story.

The weekend of my scheduled faith story quickly arrived. Friday night of that weekend, I began feeling anxious as I thought about Sunday—just two days away. So I grabbed my Bible. Without any specific Scripture in mind, I just opened it. When I did, my eyes fell on Psalm 30, "I will praise you, Lord, for you have saved me from my enemies. You refuse to let them triumph over me. O Lord my God, I pleaded with you, and you gave me my health again. You brought me back from the brink of the grave, from death itself, and here I am alive! Oh, sing to Him you saints of His; give thanks to His holy name. His anger lasts a moment; His favor lasts for life! Weeping may go on all night, but in the morning there is joy. In my prosperity I said, 'This is forever; nothing can stop me now! The Lord has shown me His favor. He has made me steady as a mountain.' Then, Lord, you turned your face away from me and cut off your river of blessings. Suddenly my courage was gone; I was terrified and panic-stricken. I cried to you, O Lord; Oh, how I pled: 'What will you gain, O Lord, from killing me? How can I praise you then to all my friends? How can my dust in the grave speak out and tell the world about your faithfulness? Hear me, Lord; oh, have pity and help me.' Then He turned my sorrow into joy! He took away my clothes of mourning and gave me gay and festive garments to rejoice in so that I might sing glad praises to the Lord instead of lying in silence in the grave. O Lord my God, I will keep on thanking you forever!"

That's *my* story! I thought to myself after reading Psalm 30. God was indeed near and personally speaking to me through that Psalm. Immediately, I was filled with praise, joy, and strength. A peace came over me, too. No longer scared, I was excited! I was excited to tell others what God had done for me. I couldn't wait for Sunday to arrive.

Sitting in the front pew that Sunday, I was surrounded by family and friends. The closer the time came for me to share my faith story, the more anxious I began to feel. Just moments before I walked to the podium, I asked Papa Don, who was sitting next to me, to pray for me. He took my hand in his and prayed.

When the sermon was over, my cue came. I left my seat and headed for the podium. At the podium, I opened my mouth to speak, and when I did an indescribable peace came over me. I was amazed. There I was, speaking in front of a large crowd, yet experiencing complete peace!

That indescribable peace that I experienced was obvious to others, too. After speaking, I talked to my neighbor who was there that Sunday morning. She told me that she couldn't believe it was actually me speaking—the one who dreaded public speaking. Someone else thought that I was a professional speaker. Me? A professional speaker?! I knew then that God had truly enabled me to do His will that day. I certainly hadn't done it on my own. I thanked God over and over for the opportunity to publicly give Him glory and praise.

Years later, I'm still being called to accomplish things that I can't accomplish on my own. But the One who calls me continues to provide me with everything I need. He always will. And if I ever forget that fact, He gently reminds me of that Sunday in July when I stood before a crowded church telling my faith story . . . basking in His indescribable peace. That peace "which transcends all understanding" (Philippians 4:7, NIV).

Beautiful Music

There I was in church listening to a small group of musicians. As I listened, I studied each musician playing his/her instruments—five women and one man. The woman playing the bass stood out to me. Not just because she was standing but because her lips were counting the measures out, as her eyes intently watched the conductor most of the time. She looked to him for timing and guidance. The other musicians would occasionally glance over at the conductor, but not as much as the woman playing the bass.

As I watched and listened, it occurred to me how much God is like a conductor in our lives. He is the one in control and the only one whose timing really matters in our lives.

Watching and listening, these questions came to my mind. Do I, like that woman who focused on the conductor, keep my eyes and heart focused on God? Or do I only occasionally look to Him for His timing and guidance? Am I playing the music that God has specifically chosen for my life? Or am I choosing my own music and arrangements? And what about my instrument? Is it out of tune? Or am I keeping it in tune through prayer, God's Word, solitude, worship and fellowship?

With my thoughts back on the string ensemble in front of me, I was amazed that such a small group of musicians could make such beautiful music. It made me think of the beautiful music we could make if each of us played our part totally focused on God, watching for His direction and timing before taking action. Beautiful music that would encourage the unbelievers around us to learn the song . . .

Gardening with God

There are times when I sense God writing a personal parable on my heart, the times He touches the ordinary objects and experiences of my life and illuminates them with heavenly meaning. Like the day He met me in the garden . . .

It was a hot summer day, and the job was before me. I had planted zinnia seeds weeks before around our ash tree in the front yard, and the newly formed garden needed weeding.

Although weeding doesn't rank among my favorite things to do, it had to be done. So, reluctantly, I gathered my garden gloves, a container, and a garden tool. Ready to begin, I sat down on the bricks surrounding the tree and garden.

Upon closer examination of the new garden, I was amazed to see how much growth there had been already. I began the tedious job of pulling the weeds out one by one. I found that some of the weeds came loose with a gentle pull and made my job easier. Others, though, had really taken root and needed more than a gentle pull. For those stubborn weeds, I needed the help of a garden tool to loosen their strong hold on the soil. Eventually, I got those tough ones out, too.

The longer I stayed at the task, the more I realized that it was sometimes hard to distinguish the weeds from the newly sprouted zinnias. So I studied the ones I knew for sure were zinnias to help me recognize the weeds "in disguise."

It was then that I felt God's Holy Spirit illuminating our garden with Heavenly meaning. The different weeds I had been pulling out began to remind me of the different kinds of sin in my life. First, I thought of the weeds that came free with a gentle pull, and I thought of daily sins that I commit—sins that have not yet taken root. For example, impatience with someone or not obeying what I felt the Spirit was nudging me to do, such as calling someone or writing a note. Next, I thought of the weeds that had taken root and how I needed the help of my garden tool to remove them. I then thought of the sins in my life that have been allowed to take root, the hidden sins in my life that I struggle with, such as judging others and greed—sins I need extra help with in irradicating. These are the sins that

God knows all about and is more than willing to help me root out. Last, I thought about how hard it was to distinguish some of the weeds in the garden from the newly sprouted zinnias, until I examined them closer. I thought about the kind of sins in my life that disguise themselves, too. Those sins that are harder to recognize without closer examination. For example, my sin of pride that at times comes disguised as self-sufficiency, or my sin of greed that comes disguised as discontentment. Those are the sins that are harder to recognize as sin. Hmm . . . .

I finished weeding our garden, and it made such a difference. Our garden finally looked like a garden instead of a weed patch. The baby zinnias had room to grown and to become all that they were meant to be, free of the weeds that sought to destroy them.

Just like our flower garden, my heart's garden needs to be weeded, too. The weeds of sin that seek to destroy me and my relationship with God and others must be removed daily. And I know that with God's help and time, my heart's garden will be all that God wants it to be. The seeds of His love have been planted in my heart already, and with His help, will mature and bloom into flowers of forgiveness, gentleness, patience, love, and more.

I am so thankful for the times God has taken the ordinary things in my life and given them Heavenly meaning. The times the ordinary is no longer ordinary because of my Master's touch.

P.S. What about those rocks in our garden, Lord? Surely there's a lesson there. Let's meet in the garden again Lord. Let's meet in the garden again . . .

A Spiritual Shower

May we be refreshed as by streams in the desert.
(Psalm 126:4)

Yikes! It was later than I thought. A quick prayer said, I bounded out of bed. No time to read the Bible, I thought to myself. No time for devotions. I was scheduled to have a paraffin treatment done in hopes of relieving sore, infamous "Minnesota cracks" on my hands. I had to get in the shower fast if I wanted to make my appointment on time.

I stood shivering outside the shower door waiting for the water to warm up. Wait a minute . . . what water? I had just turned the water on, but nothing was coming out of the showerhead. I opened the shower door again and got in the shower to check out the situation. Had Pete turned the water off earlier while working on the shower and then forgotten to turn it back on? I turned the water on again. A few dribbles of water appeared that time, but that was all.

I panicked for a moment. Would I actually have to go to the beauty salon looking like this—frizzy hair on one side of my head, plastered down on the other? Oh, no! While those thoughts raced through my mind, I fiddled with the showerhead.

Pete had just installed it, and there was obviously a glitch somewhere. I noticed a wire bar on a side of the showerhead. What was it anyway? I moved it around and when I did, the water gushed forth. Relief! Warm, precious, running water.

As I lathered up I thought about how much I take for granted every day—like running water. Thank you Lord, I prayed, for warm running water, for electricity, for indoor plumbing and heat . . . .

While showering, I also remembered the panic I felt when no water had spewed forth from the showerhead. Without the water, I couldn't get physically clean. But wait a minute. What about the water my soul needed every day? I had said a quick prayer that morning but had nonchalantly skipped my Bible reading. Why hadn't I felt panic when my soul hadn't been watered? Yet I did feel panicked at the thought of no water for a shower.

I arrived at the beauty salon on time that morning, thankful for my shower and clean hair, but I was thirsty. Spiritually thirsty.

At home, after my appointment, I went to our bedroom and spent time with God, "the Fountain of living waters" as Jeremiah 17:13 describes Him. A fountain that will never run dry or be cut off, whose life-giving waters are mine for the taking, any time, anywhere.

After spending time with God in prayer and reading His Word, my thirst was quenched and my soul refreshed. A "spiritual" shower was just what I needed . . .

A Clean House and Heart

*They hated the heavenly Light because they
wanted to sin in the darkness. They stayed away
from that Light for fear their sins would be
exposed and they would be punished. But those
doing right come gladly to the Light to let
everyone see that they are doing what God
wants them to. (John 3:20–21)*

After I cleaned our house one cloudy day, I looked around for
a few moments, enjoying my accomplishment. Things looked
"sparkly and spotless" as I surveyed my work. Like I said,
though, that was on a cloudy day . . .

The next day the sun came out, and I was shocked at my
so-called "clean" house. As I looked around, I couldn't believe
the fingerprints and dust I had missed the day before.
Without the help of sunlight, our house had seemed clean to
me but in fact wasn't.

As I thought about my "clean" house that day, I realized
that just as sunlight assists me in recognizing the dirt in our
house, so the light of God's Holy Spirit assists me in recognizing dirt in the rooms of my heart. Without sunlight or the
light of God's Holy Spirit, things may seem "sparkly and
spotless" but in fact be dirty.

Once I recognized the dirt still remaining in our home, I
got out the vacuum and dust rag—again. In no time, I
cleaned up the remaining dirt.

As for the dirt in my heart, though, I can't personally
remove it no matter how hard I try. Which reminds me of the

words of an old hymn that talks about how nothing but the blood of Jesus can wash away my sins. After confessing my sins, God's "cleaning" work of forgiveness (made possible by Jesus' shed blood at the cross for me) takes place, and the rooms of my heart become as white as snow. Just as Isaiah 1:18 tells me, "Though your sins are like scarlet, they shall be white as snow" (NIV). God forgives me, my guilt is removed and my relationship with Him is restored.

As I ponder all of these thoughts, something else occurs to me: I know that no matter how many times I clean our house, it will always need cleaning again. So it is with my heart. Daily, I need to confess my sins and ask for God's forgiveness. Until I reach Heaven, that is, where eventually my heart will *stay* clean forever. Now that's a "clean" I can't wait to survey . . .

He Is Able

Now glory be to God who by His mighty power at work within us is able to do far more than we would ever dare to ask or even dream of—infinitely beyond our highest prayers, desires, thoughts, or hopes. (Ephesians 3:20)

There we were in a parking lot in Florida—Pete, Zach and I. We were sitting in our rental car and looking through a newspaper trying to find a church we could attend the next day for Easter. We had plans for an Easter brunch with Pete's parents, and we wanted to go to church before then.

Knowing our time frame helped to reduce the number of possible churches we could attend. Yet even so, the list of options was long. While considering the options, I silently prayed, "Lord help us. Guide us to where you want us to go."

Shortly thereafter, one church location and service time stood out to us and seemed to work best for our schedule. So, together, we decided on that particular church and then headed back to the condo we had just rented.

Back at the condo, I started unpacking a few things while Pete and Zach lugged the rest of our belongings up from the car. When the two of them got back to our room, they excitedly told me that they had met the family staying in the condo right next to ours. The family had two boys, and one of them was around Zach's age. Zach was ecstatic. Pete also mentioned he had told the parents that their boys could come over to our place anytime and that they had reciprocated. "I don't know about Zach going into their condo, hon. We don't even know them . . . who they are or what they're like," I told Pete. Pete reassured me, "Zach will be just fine."

Like I mentioned earlier, Easter was the next day, and before we knew it we were sitting in a golf cart being shuttled from the parking lot to the church, the church we had decided to attend the day before.

Just inside the front door of the church, we were met by a sea of people. Somehow, we managed to get to the sanctuary. Once inside, we spotted room for the three of us near the front and we headed there. As soon as we sat down someone said "Pete!" We turned around, and Pete said, "Hi!" The people behind us beamed as Pete whispered to me, "They're our next-door neighbors at the condo—with the two boys!" Then I began beaming. I sensed God at work and I couldn't wait to meet them after the service.

Right after realizing our condo neighbors were sitting behind us, another incredible thing happened. "That's Barbie Walker over there," Pete said. Barbie Walker was John Walker's sister, and John Walker was my old boyfriend, the boyfriend who had originally introduced Pete and me years before! Pete motioned for Barbie to come over. Barbie was, of course, surprised to see us, and then asked if we had seen Connie, her sister, yet! It turned out that Connie was the receptionist at that church! Barbie told us then that Connie was probably still in the main office.

Upon hearing that, we quickly got up out of our seats and went to the office to find Connie before the service started. After we found her, we had a fun reunion full of hugs and smiles. After talking to Connie for a few minutes, we headed back to the sanctuary where Connie and her husband Jerry joined us for worship. Together, we joyfully worshipped Jesus' resurrection that Easter morning.

Later, as I considered the events of that Easter Sunday, I was reminded how much God longs to guide me in everything. Every day. Even on vacation, looking for a church. Proverbs 3:5–6 says, "Trust in the Lord with all your heart, and do not rely on your own insight. In all your ways acknowledge Him and He will make straight your paths" (NRSV). After silent prayer for guidance, God somehow supernaturally guided us (made our paths straight) as we scanned the newspaper in that parking lot in Florida looking for an Easter service to attend.

Thinking about the events of that Easter Sunday, I also considered how once we got to God's chosen destination for us that Easter Sunday, we were blessed in ways we never would have dreamed of. Which reminds me of Ephesians 3:20, which says, "(He) is able to do far more than we would ever dare to ask or even dream of." Anytime, anywhere. Even on vacation. Even if our prayers are simple, like mine was that day in Florida: "Lord, help us. Guide us to where you want us to go."

Yes, He is able. More than able to do far more than I would ever dream. Our photos of that family who stayed in the condo next door in Florida, the ones we saw that Easter Sunday at church, remind me of that truth . . .

P.S. After that Easter Sunday in Florida that we spent our remaining days of vacation on the beach with family. When it came time for them to leave, there were tears. We knew that we would miss each other deeply. We also knew that the week together was an incredible gift from God. Although they went back home to Wisconsin and we to Minnesota, we kept in touch. Years later, we are still keeping in touch. In fact, since meeting those dear friends, we have planned several Florida vacations—together!

A Tape and a House

For nothing is impossible with God. (Luke 1:37, NIV)

Buying a house was the last thing on my mind the first time I drove up to Agnes's house the summer of 1993. At the time, I was part of a group from our old church that delivered sermon tapes to shut-ins. Agnes was on my list of deliveries and visits that week. When I looked at Agnes' address I realized that I had no idea where she lived, so I called her for directions. Although I had never been in her neighborhood before, her house was easy to find. The minute I drove into her neighborhood, I liked it. Medium-sized homes, big residential lots and abundant tall, old trees—just what Pete and I had been dreaming of.

When Agnes answered the door, we introduced ourselves to each other, and she invited me in. "I like your neighborhood," I said. And I then told her that I had never been in that area before. I will always remember Agnes' quick response. "I'm selling my house. Are you interested?"

I told Agnes then about our family's plan of buying a house the following spring. For eleven years, Pete and I had been apartment and condo dwellers, and we were looking forward to that coming spring when we were hoping to buy our first home. Pete's spring sales bonus from work would make the purchase possible. Although spring seemed so far off to me then, I had already begun praying for God to guide us in our search for a house.

I ended up visiting with Agnes for quite awhile. She was such a delightful woman and so easy to talk to. I found out that she and her husband had built the house in 1946 and had raised their only child, a son, there.

The longer I stayed at Agnes' house that day, the more I started thinking about her comment to me when I first met her, the one about selling her house. And my eyes began to wander. From where I sat, I could see charming arched doorways and a separate formal dining room. The living room where we were sitting was a nice size, and a large lot with beautiful trees was right outside the picture window. Though Pete and I hadn't seriously looked at other houses yet, we knew that there were certain things we wanted in our future home: a formal dining room, a large lot, lots of trees and a porch.

I knew my curiosity was getting the best of me when I heard myself asking Agnes if I could see the rest of her house. She immediately started the tour. Besides the formal dining room, she showed me the two bedrooms on the first floor, the kitchen and the three-season porch adjoining the kitchen.

Agnes's house had everything we wanted. The more I looked, the more excited I got. I asked Agnes if I could bring Pete to see her house when he got back in town, and she agreed.

As I drove home that day, I prayed for God to reveal His will to us regarding Agnes' house.

When Pete came home from his business trip, I told him the story of Agnes' house and described it to him in detail. After listening to me I could tell he wasn't crazy about the idea. And he shared with me the fact that we wouldn't have a down payment without his spring sales bonus. He could see my excitement, though, and decided to take a look at the house anyway.

When I got Pete to Agnes' house, we weren't there for more than twenty minutes before I sensed his excitement about it, too. In fact, right then, he asked Agnes if we could bring our parents to see it!

In the following days, however, Pete kept reminding me that we didn't have a down payment and that we could never buy it without one. I remember insisting that if it were God's will for us to buy that house, He would make a way for us to get it.

Within the next week, we returned to Agnes' house with Pete's mom and dad, along with my dad. Agnes, along with her son and daughter-in-law, sat on the porch as we gave the tour to our parents.

Pete's dad was the first to speak up. He asked what price Agnes wanted for the house. When we told him, he said we couldn't go wrong and that we should buy it for sure.

After the tour, we joined Agnes and her family on the porch and told them that we were interested in buying her house. Pete offered Agnes $120,00 and she countered with $125,00. Then Pete's dad spoke up. "How about in the middle? $122,500?" Agnes accepted our offer. It was a done deal. Except for, well, you know, the minor detail—no down payment!

At that point, Pete began to explain to Agnes and her family the situation with his sales bonus, that we wouldn't have a down payment until spring. That fact didn't phase them at all! It wasn't a problem. Her son said that we could do a contract for deed until the bonus came. It was as simple as that. We left Agnes' that day a little in shock but very excited at the thought of finally owning our own home.

The next few weeks, we were busy compiling financial papers and applying for a mortgage. During that time, Pete was nervous that we might not qualify for the mortgage, but

I wasn't. By that time I was convinced it was God's will for us to buy Agnes' house and that He would work it out no matter what.

Well, God did work it out, and we moved in our new house that October—long before spring arrived and long before Pete's bonus arrived. It wasn't until later that I realized that if I had originally driven by Agnes' house and had seen a For Sale sign in the yard, chances are, I wouldn't have stopped to take a look. The house was nothing like I had imagined our future house to look like on the outside. But God knew the inside was just what we were looking for. And only He knew the perfect plan for getting me in the door. A sermon tape and a list of deliveries . . .

If something is God's will, He doesn't let anything get in the way, does He? Not a den of lions, not a king's edict, not the Red Sea, not even buying a house without a down payment. The Bible says that God's will is good and acceptable and perfect. And because of that fact, I have found that it is always worth waiting for. And sometimes, yes, sometimes, we don't even have to wait until spring.

God's Perfect Answer

Hallelujah! I want to express publicly before His people my heartfelt thanks to God for His mighty miracles. (Psalm 111:1)

It was late fall, 1997, when again I sensed God filling me with a desire to speak out publicly and tell others about what He had done in my life during my cancer journey. Every day, I was waiting expectantly for the opportunity He had in mind for me.

One day during that time, a letter arrived from our church. The church was thinking of airing some of the faith stories from past Sunday morning worship services on a local radio station. It also stated that an interview between our pastor and each faith story presenter would follow each story aired. While reading that letter, I sensed that was the opportunity God had in mind for me, and I got excited just thinking about it.

I marveled then at the changes God had brought about in me. In the past, my response would have been *far* from excited. "Me, on the radio? You've got to be kidding. No way. I don't have the voice. In fact, I've never even *liked* my voice! Speaking in front of a group is my worst nightmare. I'm definitely not the person you're looking for."

Eventually, I talked to one of our pastors and agreed to do the interview. After that initial conversation, it took about six months before any of the specifics were arranged. In June, the pastor in charge of arranging the interviews called me one day and told me that the actual taping of my faith story and interview was set up for two weeks later. Yikes! Only two weeks to go before my commitment became real.

Before the interview, I was sent a list of possible questions I would be asked during the interview. After reading the questions, I committed the interview to God in prayer and asked that the Holy Spirit would totally guide my words during the interview. I also asked friends to pray. Every day leading up to the interview, I felt strengthened by the many prayers of God's people.

The days flew by, and before I knew it, I was on my way to church for the interview. Inside the church, I found my way to the sound booth where another interview was just finishing up.

Next thing I knew, I was in the sound booth, joining our pastor. Before we started, he told me that he really didn't want to use the questions that had been provided—the ones I had received prior to the interview. Yikes! *Lord, give me the words*, I silently prayed as fear threatened to creep in and take over.

"If you make a mistake during the interview, just continue on and it will be edited later," I was told. The person who had just finished his interview also gave me some good advice. The trouble was that I couldn't remember what that good advice was the minute my interview started.

During the interview, when our pastor asked a question, I felt compelled to answer immediately. After I was asked several thought-provoking questions, which I didn't have much time to think about, the interview was over.

Driving home after the interview, my pastor's questions and the answers I had given played over and over in my mind. By the time I got home, I felt absolutely sick because of one of my answers in particular. I couldn't believe I had answered it the way I had. I was almost in tears thinking about it.

The question and answer that kept racing though my mind was, "What would you say to me or to someone you know who is diagnosed with cancer?" I had immediately answered, "Get to know the Bible. God has so much to say to us through it."

"Why had I said that?!" I asked myself on my drive home. I couldn't believe I didn't say, " to accept Jesus as your Savior and Lord of your life. *That's* the most important thing of all." I had had a chance to tell others about the importance of a relationship with Jesus, and I had blown it. Absolutely blown it.

When I told Pete about it when he came home, he tried to help. "Don't worry about it. You can always re-do it, so there's no problem. Don't worry." I listened to him, but still I felt awful.

That night in bed, I poured my heart's anguish out to God. "Forgive me, Lord, for blowing it. I don't know how it happened because I prayed for your Holy Spirit to give me the words that you wanted me to say, and others were praying, too. I feel terrible. Please forgive me, Lord." Then I drifted off to sleep.

When I awoke the next morning, that question and answer from the interview were still whirling around in my mind. I was still upset about it, but eventually I gave it to God and left it there. "Lord," I prayed, "I will trust that you can take even my mistakes and work them out to accomplish your purposes. Nothing is impossible for you, Lord." I felt much better after casting my burden on Him, and I actually began to think about other things besides that question and answer.

In the days following, God seemed so silent about the whole thing. I began to wonder if maybe it had been my enemy, Satan, who had me feel like such a failure. As I considered that possibility I was reminded of these words, "God convicts, Satan condemns."

A week later, I was reading my devotions when I came across Galatians 2: 18–19: "Rather, we are sinners if we start rebuilding the old systems I have been destroying, of trying to be saved by keeping Jewish laws, *for it was through reading the Scripture that I came to realize that I could never find God's favor by trying—and failing—to obey the laws.* I came to realize that acceptance with God comes by believing in Christ" (emphasis mine). Wow! Paul was talking here. Paul, one of the most committed followers of Jesus Christ, ever. The man who had been chosen by God to bring the good news of Jesus Christ to the Gentiles. Paul was saying in Galatians that he had come to an understanding of Christ through reading the Scriptures. Relief flooded my heart, for many people with cancer haven't yet discovered the hope and healing that lies within the pages of God's Word. At that moment I realized many people, like Paul, would find Jesus through reading the Bible.

With relief in my heart, my pastor's question returned to me, "What would you say to me or to someone you know who is diagnosed with cancer?" "Get to know the Bible. God has so much to say . . ."

God's answer, through me, was perfect after all.

The Table

Pray about everything. (Philippians 4:6)

One Sunday afternoon, Pete and I decided to go to a few garage sales. We had recently moved into our house from the condo and needed more furniture to fill the empty spaces.

Before leaving on our "furniture hunt" that day, Pete had circled a few sales from the classified section of the newspaper.

He shared with me that one of the sales was a yard sale of antiques. "It's Sunday afternoon," I protested. "The sale started Friday. They won't have anything left by now." "Let's just check it out anyway," Pete answered. So off we went.

While Pete drove, I silently prayed. "We just bought this house, Lord, and you know we don't have much money left to buy furniture for the empty spaces. Please guide us today to furniture we can afford and give us wisdom to make wise purchases."

Pete was determined to go to the yard antique sale, and he made it our first stop. When we pulled up to the sale, I was pleasantly surprised. It was still open, and there were still several antiques in the yard even though it was the last day of the sale.

When I got close enough to see some of the price tags I looked at them in disbelief—$125.00, $200.00, $125.00, $250.00. We had been in enough antique stores to know a deal when we saw one. Immediately, Pete and I spotted a dresser we liked. It was perfect for our new bedroom. The right size, the right color wood, attached mirror. Just then my thoughts were interrupted by one of the guys running the sale. "You can have it for $100.00," he told us. One hundred dollars was an incredible price for the dresser, and we quickly told him we wanted to buy it.

As Pete and the guy helping with the sale were loading the dresser into the Jeep, Pete mentioned we were also looking for an antique dining room table—a large mahogany or walnut table with carved legs. The guy thought for a moment before telling us this story . . .

The previous year, one of their neighbors had tried to give him and his brothers (who were running the sale with him that day) her dining room table. She had wanted to get rid of the table, and she knew that they were in the business of refinishing antiques and then selling them. We asked him what the table looked like. As he described the woman's table to us, it sounded exactly what we were looking for. He told us that he'd check with his neighbor to see if she still had the table and asked for our phone number so that he could give us a call regarding it.

When we finally left the yard sale with our new dresser in tow, I kept thinking about the guy's story of the table. I finally mentioned to Pete that, for some reason, I thought we needed to check with the lady right then. Pete reluctantly turned the car around and headed back to the yard sale. I got out of the car and asked the guy if there was any chance he could talk to the lady with the table yet that day. He suggested that we talk to her ourselves and showed us where she lived.

Yikes! What were we to say? "We're here regarding your free table?!" Being a salesman, I knew Pete would figure out what to say. So we drove up to her house and rang the doorbell. An elderly woman came to the door, obviously wondering who we were. Pete explained that we had just been at her neighbor's antique sale and that they had told us about her dining room table. "Is it still available?" Pete asked. "Oh, yes," she said, and invited us in to take a look at it.

The table was tucked in a small room at the back of her house. When we spotted it, Pete and I couldn't believe our eyes. It was exactly what we had in mind—a large walnut table with carved legs.

Pete asked her how much she wanted for it. "$300.00," she quickly replied. My heart sank. We had just bought the dresser for $100.00 and I knew we couldn't afford $300.00 on top of that. We thanked her for showing it to us and then headed back to the yard sale.

Back at the yard sale, we relayed to the guy and his brothers that the "free" table was now going for $300.00. "She was going to give it to us for free!" the brothers protested. "Offer her two hundred dollars and see what she says."

So back we went. When the woman answered the door again, she was surprised to find us there. When she opened the door, Pete began, "We were wondering . . . if you would take $200.00 for the table?" She thought for a moment before replying, "You can have it for $200.00 *if* you take the recliner, too. I'll show it to you."

The minute I saw the recliner, a gold leather recliner, I knew that it wasn't going anywhere near our living room, basement, or even garage! I also knew, though, that we could get rid of it . . . somehow. So we agreed to her deal and arranged a time to pick up the table and recliner. Pete and I then got in the car, stopped by the yard sale with the good news, then started the drive home for the second time that day. Our hearts were filled with excitement and thanks.

As we drove, I remembered my prayer from earlier that day. The prayer for wisdom and guidance for furniture we could afford. God had heard my prayer and He had definitely answered. He'd given us wisdom to make wise purchases and had not only guided us to furniture we could afford, but He had guided us to exactly what we were looking for.

Years later, we still have the table. Thankfully, *not* the recliner. When I look at the table these days, I can't believe it was only $200.00. At times, I have almost felt guilty for paying so little for it, but then I remember. I remember that it was God's gracious hand at work back then supplying even more than our needs through that table transaction.

I still love retelling the story of the $200.00 table, and when I do, I'm reminded of Philippians 4:6 that tells us to "pray about everything." This in turn reminds me that when God says to pray about everything, He means everything. Even empty spaces of a new family home . . .

God's Goodness

For the Lord is always good. He is always loving and kind, and His faithfulness goes on and on to each succeeding generation. (Psalm 100:5)

Pete and Zach were both busy the Sunday afternoon I decided to type some of the stories for this book. In the past, typing hadn't been easy for me because of the nerve damage in my hands caused by chemotherapy. For some reason, that Sunday I decided to try my hand at it again, hoping to see some improvement. So after lunch that day, I dug into my pile of handwritten stories, picked one and began to type.

When I was finished, I realized that I still needed to select a Bible verse, or verses, below the title. Moses' rod was referred to in the story I was working on, so I decided to use the verses that spoke of it in Exodus. I grabbed my Bible, found the desired verses, and copied them down.

Before closing my Bible, though, I noticed a circled verse, several verses below the ones I had written down. It was Exodus 4:12. I read it and then closed my Bible, not giving it much thought.

Later that same day, I got a call from Carol, my Bible study leader at church. She was wondering if I would be willing to speak at our Tuesday morning women's Bible study group, for three to four minutes, on God's goodness. She also apologized for not calling me earlier. While she spoke, it dawned on me that Tuesday was only two days away. I hesitated and she waited for my response. *How could I possibly write something in such a short time with everything else on my schedule?* I wondered. I couldn't think clearly, and so I told Carol I'd call her back. I hung up the phone, said a quick prayer and then called Deb, my faithful friend and sister-in-Christ. After listening, Deb encouraged me wholeheartedly to go for it. She told me that three to four minutes was nothing, as far as speaking goes, and that my whole life was evidence of God's goodness.

As Deb spoke, the thought came to me that maybe I could use a couple of the stories I had already written for my book. I told Deb the idea and she agreed. After our conversation, I went to look through my pile of stories, praying the whole time that God would guide me to the ones He wanted me to use.

After searching through the pile of stories, two stories stood out to me. One of them was the story I had typed earlier that day. I realized then that half of the assignment had been completed before I had even been called on by Carol to do it! I excitedly called Carol back to tell her I would be able to speak at the upcoming Bible study.

Before going to bed that night, I remembered the circled verse I had noticed while looking up the verses for Moses' rod. What had it said? I quickly looked it up again, "Now go ahead and do as I tell you, for I will help you to speak well, and I will tell you what to say" (Exodus 4:12). I knew then that God was clearly speaking. Looking back, I realized that Carol had called me with her speaking request just a few hours *after* I had read that verse!

The next day, Monday, I prayed for God's help as I wrote the introduction and conclusion for my talk on God's goodness. For the conclusion, God inspired me to include the words from the song "God Is So Good."

With God's help, I completed His assignment for me at Bible study that Tuesday. Once again I experienced His faithfulness, His goodness.

After speaking that Tuesday, I got home and went to get the mail. I was excited when I noticed a card from my dear sister-in-Christ, Linda, who lives in Wisconsin. I opened the card and read it. I smiled as I read her words, "God is so good"—the same words God had inspired me to write for the conclusion of my talk earlier that day!

As a little girl in Sunday school I learned the simple truth that "God is good," and I believed it with all my heart. Years later, I'm still like that little girl in Sunday school. I still believe that God is good. I believe it with all my heart—even when the way is scary, even when the nights are long. By the grace of God, I continue to have a childlike faith. God is so good. So good to me.

Not Home Yet

Do not conform any longer to the pattern of this world, but be transformed by the renewing of your mind. (Romans 12:2, NIV)

The movie *Titanic* was a complete smash at the box office, to say the least. Our family had talked about going to see it, but I still needed to find out if it was appropriate or not for Zach, who was ten years old at the time.

One night, we were at Jill and Greg's home, dear friends of ours. Jill mentioned to me that night that they had seen *Titanic*. I questioned Jill about the appropriateness of the movie for Zach. She strongly believed that it was not appropriate for a ten-year-old boy to see because of nudity and other factors. After hearing what Jill had to say, I agreed with her.

After my conversation with Jill, I told Zach he wouldn't be able to see the movie, after all. I told him I had no idea about the nudity and other factors. Zach was not a happy camper. According to him, *all* his friends had seen it, and some had actually seen it five or six times. He finally gave up the fight, though, once he realized how serious I was.

Several days after our *Titanic* conversation, Zach got a call from one of the girls in his group of friends with whom he hung around. A bunch of his friends were going to see *Titanic* the next weekend and she was wondering if he could go. He came to ask me if he could go or not. "No," I told him. "Why not?" he pleaded. I began to remind him then of our prior conversation regarding the movie. He was determined to go, though, and I could see that he was not going to easily settle for a no. He was mad! "*Everyone* is going, Mom, why can't I?" Again I explained. I repeated myself over and over. When he finally saw that I wasn't going to give in, he picked up the phone and told his friend that he couldn't go. After he hung up the phone, he begged me some more . . . but to no avail.

The next night, Zach got another phone call from the same friend who had called him the night before. She was calling with the same request. "No," I yelled from the basement where I was folding clothes. But his friend was determined, too, and before I knew it Zach was handing me the phone. "She wants to talk to you, Mom."

I got on the phone, and Zach's friend asked me if Zach could please go see *Titanic.* I told her no again, and I explained to her that we didn't feel it was an appropriate movie for Zach to see. She was not happy, to say the least. I handed the phone back to Zach, and he went back upstairs . . . fuming.

I was still folding clothes and praying that the Holy Spirit would guide me in what to do and say, when all of a sudden Zach appeared on the stairs . . . still angry with my decision. He applied more pressure . . . would it ever end? Was I doing the right thing? I began to wonder. Maybe it was okay for him to see the movie. The other parents obviously weren't objecting.

It was then that I felt the Holy Spirit intervening and I began to talk. I explained to Zach that as parents, we are responsible to God for our children. We're responsible for what we allow our children to do and see. I didn't feel the movie was appropriate, and I wanted to do the right thing. Not the wrong thing. Like choosing something that I knew wouldn't please God. Right before my very eyes I saw Zach's face change. Amazingly, he saw my point.

We talked some more and came to a mutual understanding—*Titanic* wasn't appropriate for him to see. Finally the arguing was over. Zach went back upstairs and while I finished folding clothes I was inspired to write a song. I raced to get some paper and a pencil to write down the words. After that I went to the piano to figure out the notes of the inspired song . . .

When the world is calling us
To accept it's point of view
Guide us by your Word, Oh Lord
And reveal to us the truth.

Chorus:
We are not home yet
We're strangers in this land
Our hearts belong to heaven
And we're trusting in God's plan

From this world, not of it, Lord
Teach our hearts not to conform
Help us be a light to all
May we truly be transformed.

(Chorus)

May the choices that we make
All bring glory unto you
Help us to resist, Oh Lord
What the world calls us to do.

(Chorus)

That song played over and over in my mind. And every time it did, I felt total confirmation from God that I had made the right decision regarding the movie.

The following weekend, the weekend that Zach had been asked to go see *Titanic*, I went to a retreat at my dear friend Tish's church. During the retreat, they had a mass. Knowing that I wasn't accustomed to attending mass, Tish asked me if I wanted to attend it or not.

Well, I decided to join Tish, and during the mass I could hardly believe it when I heard her priest say, "We need to stand out, to be peculiar, because of our faith in Jesus." Again God clearly confirmed my decision about the movie and praise welled up inside me.

Romans 12:2 says, "Do not conform any longer to the pattern of this world, but be transformed by the renewing of your mind" (NIV). According to Webster's Dictionary, to conform means "to be similar or identical" and "to act in accordance with prevailing standards or customs."

As a Christian, I am called not to conform to the world around me, but to be different. Not being different just for the sake of being different, but different because of Jesus' reign in my heart.

Hebrews 13:14 says, "For this world is not our home; we are looking forward to our everlasting home in heaven." Which reminds me again of the words from the song God inspired me with, "We are not home yet, we're strangers in this land."

As I seek to live my life according to God's rule and God's will, I will look strange to the world around me. For I will have different goals, different desires, different priorities, different morals and more. And at those times when I am tempted to fit in and to go along with the world's agenda, may God gently remind me once again that I am an alien (stranger) passing through. This world is not my home.

Emmanuel

Listen! The virgin shall conceive a child! She shall give birth to a Son, and He shall be called "Emmanuel," meaning "God is with us."
(Matthew 1:23)

I will never forget when Dennis, a singer from our former church, sang a solo one Sunday titled, "Emmanuel." I had always loved that song but had never been as moved as when I heard Dennis sing it that particular day. In the car and on my way home from church, I sang, "Emmanuel" to myself over and over again. At home, the song continued to play in my mind.

The next morning, I found myself still singing "Emmanuel"—in the shower and all throughout that day, too. Every time I had heard "Emmanuel" sung in the past, it had comforted me. For Emmanuel means, "God is with us." Yet this time was different. I couldn't figure it out. I was simply obsessed with Dennis' solo. At the time, I wondered if God was trying to get something across to me through that song.

After finding myself still singing "Emmanuel" days later, I decided that I had to write Dennis a note and tell him how moved I was by his solo.

After writing the note, I remembered thinking that it raved about his solo so much that he was going to think I was crazy! Or that I was making moves on him! So I decided I had better mention something about Pete in the note, too. After adding something about Pete, I sealed the envelope and mailed it.

The next Sunday, I spotted Dennis from a distance. I wanted to crawl in the nearest hole. Why had I sent that note? What was I thinking? I hardly knew the guy!

Yikes! After spotting me in the crowd, Dennis approached me. We greeted each other. By then I was so tongue-tied I was thankful that he spoke first. Dennis thanked me profusely for the note. At the time it seemed to me like he was going a little overboard in thanking me—after all, it was just a note. But then he explained. During that time, Dennis had been asking God whether he should continue singing or not. My note to him that week had been an answer to his prayer for guidance. God had heard his prayer and the answer was . . . yes! He was definitely supposed to continue singing. I was nearly speechless as I contemplated all that Dennis was saying.

After my conversation with Dennis that day, I began singing other songs around the house, not just "Emmanuel" anymore. For God's mission was over, He had been heard.

Like the hands of a clock, I was moved by the clockmaker Himself. Steadily. Silently. Forward. Forward . . . to the place He needed me to be, to do the things He wanted me to do. In His perfect timing. May my heart always keep time with His. Emmanuel. Yes—God is with us!

The Angry Beach Man

A gentle answer turns away wrath, but a harsh
word stirs up anger. (Proverbs 15:1, NIV)

It was another glorious day on the beach in Florida—
sunshine, light wind, eighty degrees. Pete, Zach and I were
sharing our beach spot with friends—John and Sarah, our
Italian friends from Canada; and our new Wisconsin friends,
Chris, Julie, Nicole and Tony.

We had been at the beach for some time when Pete left to
go back to the condo for a while. Chris, Julie and Nicole were
in the ocean, and Zach and Tony were back at the condo
pool. John and Sarah had gone somewhere, too. I was alone,
sitting under the umbrella, when another family moved in
next to us on the beach. They set up their chairs, spread out
their towels and took their sand toys out of a bag. Soon, they
were all set up for a fun day at the beach.

Once they were all set up, I started reading my book
again. I got thoroughly lost in it, when all of a sudden, the
dad of the newly planted family next to me started yelling at
his son. I was brought back to reality. After I listened to the
dad rant for a while, I found it hard to get into my book
again. And the more I listened, the more upset I got. My heart
ached for the child. I considered how horrible it must be to
grow up with an angry father.

I continued reading, but the dad's yelling interrupted my
thoughts again. He was yelling for his son to come and build
a sand castle with him. The son immediately joined him, only

to be yelled at again. This time his dad wanted him to go get the pail. As the child went to get the pail, he was yelled at not to bring the shovel. No matter how hard he tried, the child could not please his father.

After witnessing this whole tirade, I could hardly contain my own anger at the angry man. I wanted to yell myself! I wanted to yell, "Knock it off! Your child will never have any self-esteem after you get through with him! He is a gift from God—treat him that way!"

At that point in my thoughts, part of our group returned. I turned to Pete and told him the situation at hand. He listened to me, but soon his thoughts were elsewhere. My thoughts, on the other hand, were still on the angry beach man.

After praying, I sensed that God was calling me to talk to the angry man. At this point, my heart was pounding. I prayed for God to guide me by the Holy Spirit, to give me the words He wanted me to say, not the words I wanted to say.

I didn't want the whole group to know what I was doing, so I decided to get some money from Pete for a soda at the beachside cabana. I planned on talking to the angry beach man on my way to get a soda. God and I knew the plan, but no one else did. The angry beach man was standing a little off to the side of his family when I approached him.

Proverbs 15:1 says, "A gentle answer turns away wrath, but a harsh word stirs up anger" (NIV). I found myself face to face with the angry beach man when I spoke these words quietly and gently. "Jesus can help you with the anger." At that moment, looking into the angry beach man's eyes, I felt compassion. It was obvious he was controlled by his anger, a slave to it. Jesus was the only one who could truly set him free. I knew that God had indeed given me those words to say.

After I spoke, I was prepared to run! But the angry beach man threw his arms down next to his sides and said, "Humph!" He then turned and walked away. "A gentle answer turns away wrath."

After my encounter with the angry beach man, I walked away, knowing I had been obedient to God. I had done what He had called me to do that day on the beach. I never would have attempted it, though, without God's direction.

Maybe my words to that man were the first seeds of truth that had ever been planted in his angry heart. Or maybe the hundredth. Whichever was the case, I prayed that many more seeds would be planted there, and that one day he would know God's love for him and the freedom that only Jesus offers.

I prayed for the child of the angry beach man, too. I prayed that he would come to know that his Heavenly Father is so unlike his earthly father. His Heavenly Father loves him just the way he is . . . weaknesses and all. I prayed that he would come to know God's unconditional love, and His Son, Jesus Christ.

As a Christian, I am Jesus' representative, a light of His love and His grace—at school, at home, at work, at the beach. I need to plant seeds of His love wherever I go, and I need to daily obey the promptings of the Holy Spirit. Even if it means coming face to face with an angry beach man.

Lessons in the Sand

It was our last day of vacation at Vanderbilt Beach in Naples, Florida, and it was windy. I mean windy. Too windy for beach umbrellas, hats, towels, even people—there just weren't many others around.

Like I said, it was our last day of our beach vacation. We were determined to stay beachside even if the sand was stuck to our bodies, head to toe, like flies on flypaper. Windy or not, we wanted to make the most of our last day. At one point, I asked Pete if he wanted to go for a walk down the beach and he agreed. Zach decided to join us, along with our friend Sarah. So the four of us started walking down the beach on our usual route. Soon, we realized the wind was just too much to take head on, so we decided to turn around and head the other direction.

On our walk, we were all unusually quiet. Each of us seemed to be soaking it all in—the wind, the waves, the cool salty air—plus the fact that it was our last day.

As we walked, my mind began to wander, as it usually does on beach walks. I began to silently pray. I even prayed that I would find a big shell. I'm embarrassed to say I prayed for such an inconsequential thing, but hey, the Bible says in Philippians to pray about everything, right?! (Phil 4:6)

I had no more than finished my "shell" prayer when a woman we didn't know came up to us. She told the four of us that if we wanted some shells we should go to where she was pointing, which was several yards up the beach. Others were already shelling there. Excited, we headed to the spot.

As soon as we got to where the shell-seekers were, we immediately knew that we had never seen anything like it in our lives. Because of the wind that day, the waves were wildly crashing on the shore and literally cutting ridges into the sand, exposing shell after shell. The wild waves were also bringing in hordes of shells from their homes farther out in the ocean. Shells, shells, and more shells were right at our feet.

The four of us joined the shell-seekers in gathering shells as fast as we could. I suggested to Zach that he collect enough shells for everyone in his class back home. In no time, he had more than twenty-five beautiful conch shells lying on the beach.

Looking at his pile of shells, though, we realized that we had a major problem. We hadn't brought a bag along on our walk. How would we ever get that many shells back to our spot on the beach? As we pondered the bag problem, Sarah said that she had some bags back at our spot and graciously offered to go and get them.

At one point, in awe, I exclaimed, "Can you believe God's creation, Zach?!" He didn't answer. He was too busy shelling.

I knew that I was limited in the number of shells I could bring home, so I was very picky about which ones to collect that day. Even so, my hands were soon full. As I reached down for one more shell, another shell fell out of my hand.

It was then I heard God speaking silently but clearly to my heart. There I was with both hands full of shells, yet I was reaching for more. It was so typical of my life at times. Full hands . . . yet wanting more. Full closet . . . yet wanting more. Full house . . . yet wanting more. Full vacation . . . yet wanting more. Right then and there I asked God for forgiveness for my discontentment, for my greed. His forgiveness washed over me like the waves of the ocean, and my heart then filled with thanks for His many daily blessings—including the "shell extravaganza."

Sarah eventually returned with the bags, and we filled them to the top with our collected shells. On the way back to our spot on the beach, the waves brought an unusually beautiful shell and laid it right at my feet—a brilliant coral-colored shell. I had never seen such a gorgeous shell. The color was simply striking. I reached for it and picked it up. I had it in my hands, but only for a short time before the wild waves carried it away again. I tried to find the shell, but to no avail. I was disappointed I had lost it. But then, within a few steps, I found an even more magnificent shell than the coral one. I reached for it and held it securely. I was determined to hold on to this one.

Again God spoke to my heart. How many times had I been disappointed about something in my life, only to find out that right around the corner God had something even better awaiting me?

On the way back to our spot, I trailed behind the others. I was thinking about a lot of things, including my earlier "shell" prayer. I had asked for a single big shell that morning, and God had supplied a multitude of shells—more than we had ever seen in one place—more than I would have ever imagined. It reminded me of Ephesians 3:20, "Now glory be to God who by His mighty power at work within us is able to do far more than we would ever dare to ask or even dream of—infinitely beyond our highest prayers, desires, thoughts, or hopes." And I thought to myself then, My prayers are too small, Lord. My prayers are too small.

Although it's been awhile since that windy day at the beach, I still think about the "shell lessons." When disappointment comes knocking, I remember the coral shell, which reminds me that God's surprises are right around the corner. And believing that with all my heart, I am filled with hope. When greed or discontentment comes knocking, I remember my hands full of shells, reaching for more, and I am reminded to find my contentment in God alone.

Other times, God reminds me of the "shell extravaganza" to remind me to pray big prayers. For God is able. Nothing is impossible for Him, not even taking a cool, windy, last day of vacation on the beach and turning it into a glorious day. A day to remember . . .

A Saying, a Pamphlet and a Streetcar

God desires everyone to be saved and to come to the knowledge of the truth. (1 Timothy 2:4, NRSV)

Weeks before a scheduled New Orleans business trip I planned to take with Pete, these words from a devotional pamphlet came to mind. "You've called us Lord to witness, called to speak of your dear Son. Holy Spirit grant discernment, lead us to some seeking one." The closer we got to the trip, those words came to mind more frequently. I was filled with anticipation as I sensed God at work although at the time, I was unsure of His plans.

Upon arriving in New Orleans, I was thrilled to find out that my daytime companions, Audrey and Joyce, were both Christians. Audrey was the wife of Pete's boss; Joyce was the wife of Pete's client. Audrey, Joyce and I immediately connected when we met, and our days together were filled with sightseeing, shopping, sharing our faith, eating and laughing. Our husbands couldn't believe the intensity of our love for each other in just a few short days. Discussing that fact at dinner one night, we proceeded to tell them, "Well, we're sisters! Sisters-in-Christ!"

One night during dinner, someone from our group suggested we go hear a famous trumpet player perform during one of our nights in New Orleans. Everyone thought it was a great idea. Everyone except for me, that is. As a cancer survivor, I didn't relish the thought of listening to a musician in a smoky bar. But since everyone else was so enthusiastic about the idea, I agreed to go along.

The night of the scheduled concert, our whole group had dinner together. After dinner, we found our way to the club. Upon entering the club, we soon found ourselves in a very narrow, smoky and crowded stairwell, trying to make our way to the second floor, where the concert was scheduled to take place.

While bodies around me were pushing and shoving, trying to get up the stairs, something caught my eye. There on the stairwell landing was a pamphlet. Although I was being physically pushed up the stairs by the crowd, I was determined to see what the cover of that pamphlet said. So I turned around and glanced at it again. When I did, I read,

"Will you accept Jesus as your personal Savior?" I couldn't believe it! *You are here, Jesus, even in this smoky, crowded place,* I thought to myself.

Upstairs at the club, I wondered if there was a possible connection between the saying that had come to me prior to, and during, our trip: "You've called us Lord to witness, called to speak of your dear Son. Holy Spirit grant discernment, lead us to some seeking one" and the pamphlet on the stairwell. I didn't think about it a whole lot more, though, once the concert began. I got caught up in the music and fun instead. We had a great time listening to the music, and I was glad I had gone along with the group. After the concert, we made our way back to the hotel and said our goodbyes for the night.

The next morning, Joyce, Audrey and I decided to take a ride on the famous New Orleans streetcar named "Desire" and to do a little exploring. So we left the hotel on foot, walked to the streetcar stop and waited for it to arrive. By that time, my feet were killing me. My new shoes had caused blisters, and I was anxious to sit down.

Unfortunately, the streetcar was jam packed when it arrived, and we all had to stand for a few blocks. When someone finally got off, Joyce and Audrey motioned for me to sit down. I jumped at the chance because of my sore feet. Even though we only had a few more blocks to ride before getting off, sitting was a welcome relief.

During our short streetcar ride, I didn't look at the person next to me until our scheduled stop was in view. When I reached to ring the bell for our stop, I glanced over and saw that my seat companion was an older African

American woman. I also noticed then that she was holding a pamphlet in her hands. I couldn't believe my eyes. She was holding the exact same pamphlet I had seen the night before at the club where we had heard the concert, the pamphlet that asked readers if they would receive Jesus as their personal Savior! What was I to do?! The next stop was our stop. I knew I didn't have much time. "Guide me, Lord," I quickly prayed.

When I got up from my seat, I said to the woman next to me, "I see your pamphlet." "Yes," she said. "Say yes," I added as I got up from my seat. Then, as I approached the door of the streetcar to get off, I turned around and looked at that woman again. "I will," she said and smiled. I smiled and descended the stairs. I couldn't wait to tell Joyce and Audrey the *whole* story that had begun weeks earlier, back in Minneapolis . . .

A coincidence? No way. Not when viewed through an eternal lens. Rather, a part of God's plan, which according to Romans 12:2 is "good, acceptable, and perfect" (NRSV).

Isaiah 55:9 says, "For just as the heavens are higher than the earth, so are my ways higher than yours and my thoughts than yours." I constantly marvel at God and His wonderful higher ways—how He can work out the details of my life, the details of other's lives, and then weave them together creating a beautiful tapestry of His love.

Like I mentioned earlier, the streetcar that Joyce, Audrey and I rode on in New Orleans was named "*Desire.*" What a perfect place to say yes to Jesus—the One, the only One who can completely satisfy our longings; our desires. The One whose desire still is "to seek and to save the lost" wherever they may be. Even in a crowded, smoky stairwell of a bar—or on a streetcar named "Desire."

Westy's Solo

The Lord is close to those whose hearts are breaking. (Psalm 34:18)

It was an evening in late November of 1998 when Zach, his friend Westy, and I were driving to the hospital. We were on our way to visit Zach's grandpa, my dad.

Prior to that evening, Westy's mom had told me that he was going to be featured in area Christmas concerts. So on the way to the hospital that evening, we talked about his upcoming singing engagements. Westy's voice was like none I had ever heard, and he was only nine years old. As I drove, I told Westy that his voice was a "gift from God" and that "God must be so pleased that you're using it."

The thought occurred to me of having Westy sing at the hospital for Dad, during our visit that evening. He agreed, and I asked him then what song he'd like to sing. Right away he answered, "The song from *Titanic*." I considered his choice for a moment and thought about how Dad hadn't seen the movie *Titanic* and that he wouldn't be familiar with the song. So I asked Westy if he knew any Christmas songs he could sing instead. (Thinking it would be more meaningful for Dad.) "No, I want to sing the *Titanic* song," Westy told me. He was clearly determined to sing that song, and so I agreed.

A short time after we arrived at the hospital, I told Dad that Westy had a song to sing for him. So right there in Dad's room, Westy began to sing the theme song from the movie *Titanic*, "My Heart Will Go On." As he sang for Dad, strangers began gathering at the door of Dad's room, anxious to see whose voice was spilling into the hallway.

Everyone thoroughly enjoyed Westy's singing so much that when he was through with the *Titanic* song, I asked him if he could sing some more. He agreed and began singing some Christmas songs from his upcoming concerts. Dad and the gathered crowd were clearly delighted.

We had no way of knowing the night of Westy's impromptu concert that Dad would pass away two nights later. And when he did, we realized how appropriate Westy's first song had been the night of his hospital "concert" for Dad.

The night Dad passed away, Pete and I both had our cars at the hospital. Zach and I rode home together, and Pete drove home separately. On the way home, Zach turned to me and said, "Mom, I have a great idea. Westy should sing that song at Grandpa's funeral." I told him immediately that I thought it was a great idea, too.

Days later Westy did indeed sing at Dad's funeral. And as we all listened carefully to the words of "My Heart Will Go On," we were deeply touched. God's hand was clearly evident.

The week following Dad's funeral was Zach's sixth grade band concert. Pete was out of town, so I went alone and sat with friends. At the concert, we were given programs, which I used throughout the concert to follow along. Towards the end of the concert, Zach's band teacher announced that although it wasn't in the program, one of the students would be playing a solo—the theme song from *Titanic*! Another child. Same song. I could hardly believe it!

Psalm 34:18 says, "The Lord is close to those whose hearts are breaking." By faith I believed that the Lord was close to me as I grieved the loss of my dad, but I was so thankful for the tangible evidence that He sent that night through a simple song. Evidence that whispered, "I am here. I am here."

As the student played, tears filled my eyes. Joy and peace sprung up inside. God had seen my heartache. God was near. Right then, my heart began singing its own song of faith. And while harmonizing with God's grace, I knew that *my* heart would go on . . .

Needs or Desires?

And my God will meet all your needs according to His glorious riches in Christ Jesus.
(Philippians 4:19, NIV)

As I waited in line at a local print shop, Zach went to snoop around. Before I knew it, he was back with an oversized glue stick in his hand. "Can I get this?" he asked me. "Don't you have any glue sticks?" "No," he answered. "Not even at school?" I questioned, knowing that in the one month since school had started, not one glued project had come home. "Well, yeah, at school. Can't I get this?" "No," I said. So Zach reluctantly went to put it back on the rack.

After a short time, Zach was back at my side again, this time holding a padlock. *When did they start selling padlocks at the print shop?!* I wondered. "Can I get this?" he asked. "Tim and I could share it for our locker. People are stealing things from school. I know people have gone through my desk because things are rearranged. "Really?" I asked. "Really." As he held the padlock, I noticed the $7.99 price tag. "We'll have to talk to Dad. He might have one you could use. *Or else we'll get a cheaper one someplace else*, I thought to myself. "That one's $7.99," I said. "Oh," he said, and realizing I wasn't going to give in, he went to put it back on the rack, too.

After Zach put the padlock back, he returned empty-handed. But there was a rack with assorted pens right next to where we were standing. Sure enough, he noticed them and pulled a marker off the rack. "I really need this, Mom." "You do?" I asked. "You don't have any like that?" "Well I do, but they're both dried up." "What do you use them for?" I continued. "Lots of things . . . at school." "Okay, you can get one," I told him.

Pulling out of the print shop's parking lot that day, I realized how much I must sound like Zach when I talk to my heavenly Father.

How many times had I asked God for something that wasn't a true need? I may even have had something similar to what I was asking for already but was just not content with what I had. To those requests, God sometimes looks into my heart and says, "No."

I then thought about how many times I had asked God for one thing and got another, and how God sometimes says, "Not now," although eventually He fulfills my request at a later date.

Finally, I considered the times I had gone to God with a real need, totally depending on Him. The times when He had looked into my heart, recognized the need and then graciously supplied it.

It's funny how as an adult I can sound just like my child at times. And sometimes I wonder who the real teacher is. We teach our children, but at times, they teach us even more. Like the day at the print shop, waiting in line . . .

A Job Especially for Me

Others may do a greater work
But you have your part to do;
And no one in all God's heritage
Can do it as well as you.
(Streams in the Desert)

Another year. Another trip. Back to our favorite family destination—Florida. This particular Florida trip, Pete, Zach and I were at the beach for two weeks. Two wonderful weeks. Looking back, one day stands out above all the rest. That memorable day we were at the beach with our new friends, Tom, Linda and their two boys, Stephen and Andrew.

It was late afternoon when, all of a sudden sirens broke the silence around us. Looking to our right, we saw fire trucks, police cars, and paramedics arriving at the beach.

The emergency crews quickly emerged from their vehicles and spread out all along the beach, their eyes searching the water. A sickening feeling came over us as we learned they were looking for someone who had been reported missing by a friend. At that moment in time, it seemed that all eyes were scanning the water for a sign of life.

It was then I noticed him. He was sitting on the beach with his face in his hands. He looked around twenty years old. The police talked to him for a few moments before they, too, began to search.

Zach's crying interrupted my thoughts. He was frantic at the thought of someone drowning. "If they pull a dead person out of the water, I'm never coming to the beach again," he told us. Pete said he would walk Zach back to the condo we had rented. After Pete and Zach left, my gaze turned once again to the man in his twenties, the man the police had talked to. He was all alone. While watching him, I learned that he was the one who had called for help. My heart broke for him. I could only imagine the horror that was his at that very moment. Someone he knew, a friend, was gone, possibly dead.

I had to talk to him. I had to say a prayer for him. "God, please save his friend," I begged over and over. "You know where he is right now. Please reveal it to us."

It was then that our new friends, Tom, Linda, Stephen and Andrew, decided to leave the beach, too. They wanted to get out of the blazing sun for the day. What was going on? I didn't get it. I was surrounded by Christians but no one else seemed to really care about the situation around us. By then, my own heart was rapidly beating, and I knew I had to somehow help.

I said goodbye to our friends and started walking towards the man whose friend was missing. He was still sitting when I approached him, his head hung low. He looked up as I drew near. Face to face with him, I saw that his eyes overflowed with tears, his face wrought with distress. "I'm really sorry. Is it your friend who's missing?" I gently questioned. He proceeded to tell me that, yes, it was his friend, and they had been out in the ocean together. Later, when he had gotten out of the ocean, he was unable to locate his friend. He naturally feared the worst—that his friend had drowned.

I told him that I was begging God to save his friend and was asking God to show us where he was. "God knows exactly where he is. He'll show us," I told him. I said that I would keep praying and then I headed back to my earlier spot on the beach. Amazingly, within five minutes, the friend was found . . . alive! It turned out that he had been walking on the beach when he learned that all the commotion was for him! I praised God instantly—his friend was alive! God *had* shown us where he was. As I gathered the rest of our belongings on the beach, I pondered all that had happened. I remembered my family and friends leaving. I remembered my pounding heart and the thought that God knew where the friend was. I remembered the sad friend and thought about how happy he must have been at the good news.

Walking back to the condo I wondered why I had felt so compelled to talk to the sad friend. His friend was really okay. Alive. Unharmed. I began to question whether my actions were truly guided by the Holy Spirit; if they were truly God's plan.

When I got to the condo, I quickly relayed the story to Pete and Zach. Afterwards, when Pete took a shower, I sat down on the couch, exhausted. There on the coffee table in front of me was a *Guidepost* magazine, and I picked it up. I turned to a story written by one of the editors. I had read and enjoyed stories by that editor before and was anxious to read another one of her stories. The story was about a time the editor had helped a poor skunk. The skunk had somehow gotten an empty yogurt container stuck on himself and the editor had helped to remove it. She concluded the story by saying "that every now and then, God's answer to a need, is me."

I finished that story with a smile on my face. Through that story, God confirmed to me that I had done what He had called me to do. His plan had been accomplished. He hadn't called Pete, Zach, Tom, Linda, Stephen or Andrew for the job that day. No wonder they hadn't felt the urgency, like I had, to do something. For some reason known only to God, it had been a job made especially for me.

Remembering that day on the beach and the possible drowning, two thoughts occur to me. The first is that many are spiritually drowning in the unbelieving world around me and, I wonder, am I as distraught over those who are spiritually drowning as that guy on the beach was when he thought his friend was physically drowning? And when opportunities arise, do I share the lifesaving truth of Jesus Christ with them in hopes that they too will be spiritually saved?

The second thought that occurred to me is that I need to ask God to daily guide me by His Holy Spirit. To show me the jobs He has especially for me, whether on the beach, at home, or at school. Jobs that no one else can do, jobs in accordance with His perfect plan.

P.S. My mom died in 1985. After my dad died in 1998, we brought many of their "treasures" home in boxes and put them in our attic. The day after editing the preceding beach story and writing the ending for it, I was sorting through some of those treasures and came across several poems and sayings that my mom had torn out of publications and saved over the years. I began reading them. One in particular almost took my breath away. Typed and torn around the edges, yellowed from age, it said:

Others may do a greater work
But you have your part to do;
And no one in all God's heritage
Can do it as well as you.

Who but God could arrange for me to read that poem when I did—almost sixteen years after my mom's death, years after she had torn it out. A day after editing the beach story and writing the ending to it.

A few years later, and through that poem, God again confirmed my role on the beach that day of praying and talking with the distraught young man who thought his friend was drowning.

Others may do a greater work
But you have your part to do;
And no one in all God's heritage
Can do it as well as you.

That simple poem touched my mom's heart at one time enough for her to tear it out and save it. Years later, it touched mine. They are encouraging words for this time and this place. Thank you, Mom, and thank you, God, my Heavenly boss, who writes my job descriptions and knows just where to find me. Even when I'm on the beach. Miles from home . . .

P.S.S. Months after writing this story, I tried to find the original magazine article mentioned. I wanted to make sure I had quoted the words from the article correctly. I searched high and low, but I couldn't find the article, even after praying for God's help in locating it.

Finally, I called the magazine's customer service department and explained what I was looking for and an approximate date, but I didn't know the name of the article. The woman on the other end took down the information and said she would forward it to the right person. She also told me to call back in December if I hadn't heard back from them. December came and I still hadn't heard anything, so I called Customer Service again. Still nothing showed up. Then one day, I went to Nannette's for tea. (See the story titled, "Tea, a Belated Gift and More.")

Summer Project 1997

*Then I told them about the desire God had put
into my heart. (Nehemiah 2:18)*

While studying the book of Nehemiah during a women's Bible study at our church, I was especially drawn to one certain fact about Nehemiah, the man chosen by God to lead the people in the rebuilding of Jerusalem's walls. Tucked into chapter two of Nehemiah's story is the simple fact that God had put a desire into Nehemiah's heart to rebuild Jerusalem's walls.

Day after day, I found myself pondering that fact from Nehemiah's life, and one day I found myself personalizing it. I told myself that God could fill *my* heart with His desires;

His plans for me, just like He had filled Nehemiah's so many years before. And I began praying that He would. I was anxious to see what specific desires God would plant in my heart. At the time, I was ready and waiting expectantly on God. Little by little, God made His desires for me become clear. In His perfect way. In His perfect time.

A short time after I began praying about God's specific desires for me, I began to feel a strong desire to do something with Zach and some of the kids around our neighborhood during the upcoming summer vacation. Although it wasn't immediately clear to me exactly what God wanted me to do, I continued praying and continued watching for His answer.

A couple ideas came to mind one day. One idea was for the kids and me to visit a local nursing home once a week to encourage the residents. The other idea was for me to start a weekly Bible study with Zach and the neighborhood kids.

As I began praying about these ideas, however, I didn't feel any confirmation from God that either of them was truly God's plan for me, for us. So I abandoned those ideas and continued praying.

One day, a short time later, a third idea popped into my mind—to get together with the neighborhood kids once a week during the summer and to make various craft projects. *How fun!* I thought to myself. *What purpose would that accomplish, though?* I silently wondered. Right then and there, as I prayed over that third idea, another thought came to me. Maybe we could sell the kids' handmade crafts at the end of the summer and then donate the profits to a local charity. The name of a local charity came to mind then, too—Sharing and Caring Hands, a wonderful Minneapolis charity that helps the homeless with their needs.

I began at once to bathe those new ideas in prayer. But again God seemed silent. So silent, in fact, that I started to become frustrated. One day I prayed, "God, please let me know if this is your desire; your plan for the kids and me. I don't want to organize this project if it's not your will. I need to know if I should start planning for it or not. School is almost out. Please let me know." Amazingly, His answer to that prayer came within twenty-four hours . . .

The next day, our family had planned to go boating on Lake Minnetonka with some friends of ours. Driving to the lake, we noticed clouds starting to roll in and we hoped they would pass. But by the time we got to the lake and met our friends, it started to rain.

Pete suggested we all go to the coffee shop across the street for a cup of coffee. He thought that maybe the clouds would pass if we gave it some time.

It was a Saturday morning, and the coffee shop was over-flowing with people. We spotted an open table outside, though, and our group went inside in shifts to order. I was the last of our group to go inside and order. I waited and waited and waited, and then waited some more. By the time I finally got my order and got to our table outside, the weather was improving.

After I sat down, I noticed that everyone else was either done or almost done with their treats. Pete suggested that he and Mark could go and get the boat ready and that the rest of us could meet them in ten minutes or so. The plan sounded good, so they left for the boat. After they left, I began eating my muffin.

Within minutes of the guys leaving, a couple walked by our table. As my eyes followed them, I immediately recognized the woman. I could hardly believe my eyes! Her name was Mary Jo Copeland, the woman responsible for starting and running Sharing and Caring Hands. This was the charity that had come to my mind the day before when I had considered giving the proceeds of the kids' summer project to a local charity.

After seeing Mary Jo Copeland, no doubt remained within me. I knew God was saying, " Yes! Yes! Yes! It is my desire, my plan for you to work with the kids this summer— to make craft projects with them, to sell the projects and then to give the proceeds to Sharing and Caring Hands." It seemed that my heart did somersaults as I watched Mary Jo Copeland continue down the sidewalk. My heart overflowed with praise in the face of answered prayer. And I realized then that the earlier rain had been for a purpose—so had the extra-long wait for my muffin and the outside table we had gotten.

P.S. The kids and I were all blessed more than I could have ever imagined as we worked on that 1997 summer project. When we finished, the kids asked if we could do it again the next summer. I told them I had to pray about it. I had to know if it was God's plan for us or not. For I had learned that God doesn't give us His supernatural strength for uncommanded work. After praying over a period of time, I didn't feel God leading us to do it again the following summer.

By the grace of God, I listened and obeyed. When that next summer arrived, my dad was sick with cancer and living with us. Then I was diagnosed with my second cancer. God knows best . . . always. Two years later, though, God did call me to do the summer project with the neighborhood kids once again, in the summer of 1999. Once again, God was faithful through it all. Once again, we were blessed.

To this day I am still thankful for Nehemiah's story where I discovered that God put a desire into his heart for rebuilding Jerusalem's walls. Since discovering that simple fact, I have prayed many times for God to put His desires into my heart, and He has. For He knows His desires and His plans for me. (Jeremiah 29:11) All I need to do is ask, trusting that He will let me know, trusting that He will bring it to pass. In His perfect time. In His perfect way. For as Psalm 138:8 says, "The Lord will fulfill His purpose for me" (NIV).

A Little Shed Named "Soul Purposes"

I am the Lord, the God of all mankind; is there anything too hard for me? (Jeremiah 32:27)

I was talking with my sister-in-Christ, Jill, one day when she mentioned that she thought God had a plan for the two of us—some sort of ministry that we could do together. I, too, had had that same thought before, and as Jill and I talked that day, I remembered another sister-in-Christ who had also thought God had a plan for Jill and me. As Jill and I began to talk about ministry possibilities and wondered if the possible ministry would have anything to do with joy, since others frequently commented on our "joy in the Lord," we agreed to pray about it. That was in January of 1999.

By the end of April, God had not made it clear that He had a ministry for Jill and me. It had been fun thinking about the possibility, but it just didn't seem like God's will at that point. But then came May, the May when I had been praying for God to show me how He wanted me to use the rest of the money I had allotted for His special purposes from an inheritance I had received—$2,000.00.

One Friday night during May of 1999, Pete had rented a movie for the two of us. Zach and his friend were at a church concert, and it was one of those rare opportunities when Pete and I could watch a movie uninterrupted.

In the movie, one of the main characters owned a charming little store. I was reminded of the charming specialty stores where I had worked in the past. As I watched the main character at work in her store, I said to Pete, "I'd love to own my own store." After those words left my mouth, I wondered where in the world they had come from?!

While attending the University of Minnesota years ago, I had dreamt of owning my own store—until that is, I worked retail for a while. By the time I left the retail world when Zach was four years old, I remembered thinking to myself that I would never work retail again.

When I woke up the next day, the store idea was still on my mind. The thought occurred to me that maybe Jill and I could open a store. Maybe God had a plan for the two of us after all.

The more I thought about the store idea though, the crazier it seemed. Although I had come a long way since my colon cancer, nine months earlier, I knew that opening and running a store would do me in. I knew that I simply didn't have the energy that a retail operation would require. Yet, the store idea persisted.

The Tuesday after I had watched that movie with Pete, another sister-in-Christ, Jeanne, was at our house for our weekly Bible study. When we finished our study, we began talking about what we had done the weekend before. Jeanne mentioned that she had gone to a movie and then I mentioned we had rented one. I then told Jeanne about the store idea and how it had evolved from watching the movie. The two of us then started talking about store possibilities. She suggested a boutique in our home, like one of our mutual acquaintances occasionally had. I told her that my sister-in-law had had a boutique of my artwork one year at her house. I then suggested a "store" on our porch. Next, a thought came to me of a store in our backyard. After Jeanne left that day, I had fun considering the backyard "store idea." I remembered a tiny, tiny store that had operated behind a clothing store where I had once worked. I remembered how small it was and how adorable it was. Hmmm . . .

The next morning, I was vacuuming, getting the house ready for out-of-town company the following weekend. As I worked, I was still considering different options for the store idea when all of a sudden a thought exploded in my mind. It was a whole new concept. We could take a tool shed and turn it into a charming retreat for prayer, fellowship, reading, and an occasional boutique of handmade Christian gifts—in our backyard! A place where friends could spend time alone or with others. A place where spiritual purposes could be accomplished. Then I remembered—I remembered the prayer I had been praying. The prayer in which I had been asking God to show me His plans for the $2,000.00 from my inheritance.

I was still vacuuming when I remembered a picture and an article that I had seen at my brother and sister-in-law's home in Florida, years earlier. The picture I remembered was of a regular storage shed that had been converted into a charming storage shed. I had torn the article out way back then but didn't know if I still had it or not.

With the tool shed on my mind, another sister-in-Christ, Pat, called. I shared the quiet retreat idea with her. By then I was so excited about the idea I couldn't help but share it with her. Pat listened carefully and was very encouraging. She said that she'd join me in prayer regarding the idea.

After talking to Pat and eating lunch, I began calling stores to get an idea of how much storage sheds cost. The prices were reasonable, and my excitement grew.

Once I got an idea of how much storage sheds cost, I decided to see if I by any chance still had that picture from Florida of the converted shed, the one I had remembered earlier while vacuuming. I doubted I still had it, considering how long ago it had been, but I asked God to help me find it if I still had it, and I went downstairs to look. I opened our file cabinet and about five minutes later found the article!

I was amazed I still had the picture, and I was delighted to see that the converted shed was as charming as I had remembered it. The size of the pictured shed was eight-foot by eight-foot. I went and measured an eight-foot by eight-foot spot on our porch so that I knew what size I'd be working with. I realized then that an eight-foot by eight-foot shed would hold more than two people, which I had originally imagined. An eight-foot by eight-foot shed could hold a small Bible study *group*!

It was late afternoon that same day when I got a call from my brother who lives in Florida. We talked about our late father's estate, and I told him I was going to send him a check for his half of the remaining money in Dad's checking account. My brother was quick to say that he and my sister-in-law wanted to give me $1,500.00 of their half of the remaining money. He said that they wanted me to use it for a trip or whatever I decided. He said it was for all of the running around and more I had done for Dad before he passed away. I told my brother then that I wasn't expecting anything for what I had done for Dad. He said that they wanted to give me the money. We went back and forth, and finally I accepted their gift, sensing God's hand at work. *Would the prayer and Bible study shed cost $2,000.00 plus my brother and sister-in-laws $1,500.00 gift?* I wondered . . .

After my conversation with my brother, I called Jill. I was bursting with excitement over God's possible ministry plan, a plan possibly for the two of us. It turned out that the weekend before (the same weekend that the store idea had come to me) she had told her husband that she thought the two of us should open a store together. I told Jill about the converted shed idea. Her excitement and interest were evident. We had so much fun that day, talking about the possibilities. She, too, said that she would join me in prayer regarding the idea.

I called Pat back to tell her of the $1,500.00 gift from my brother and sister-in-law and my conversation with Jill. I also mentioned that an eight-foot by eight-foot shed could hold a small Bible study *group*, something I hadn't thought possible when I talked to her earlier that day. Pat then told me that she had been cleaning after our earlier conversation and had found some old Bible study guides. Instead of throwing them away, she had given them to her husband to put somewhere. She had told him that I might want them!

The following day, I talked to Deb, another sister-in-Christ. I told Deb that I had an idea I wanted to share with her and that I wanted her to tell me if she thought I was crazy or not. After sharing the prayer shed idea with Deb, she related the following:

The weekend before, on her way home from church, she had been looking at all the homes along the way. Deb said that she had pictured herself living in one of those homes. If she did live there, she would put up a small shelter, like a bus shelter, where people driving by could stop and pray if they wanted to. She had wondered at the time where that idea had come from! But after hearing about the shed idea she felt that her experience might have been confirmation for what I was sensing God calling me to do. God was at work. He was definitely at work . . .

The following week, Jill and I went to look at sheds together. We wanted to see exactly what was available, the cost involved and also what it would take to assemble the shed. We found a couple of assembled sheds at one of the stores and picked up brochures on other styles that could be special ordered.

As we looked through the special order brochures, we were immediately drawn to a miniature pine cabin design. We both thought it was absolutely charming and, although expensive, we probably had enough money in our fund for it. We needed to add up the window cost, shingles, and other supplies to determine if the shed we loved would fall within our budget, which, after my brother and sister-in-law's gift, was $3,500.00. Jill and I were excited!

The following week, I didn't feel well. I was very bloated and weak. I waited a couple of days before calling my oncologist, but on Wednesday I called her office and talked to my nurse. After talking with my doctor, the nurse ordered a CT scan for the following Friday and then scheduled a follow-up appointment for Monday.

During that time, I was feeling so rotten, I seriously wondered if the cancer was back. *Why would God give me the prayer shed idea, though, if I wouldn't be able to complete it?* I thought to myself.

Friday, I had the scheduled CT scan of my pelvic area and abdomen. It was a scan that I had had many times before since my original cancer diagnosis in 1991. That Friday's scan was different, though. The technician scanned the whole area, and then another technician came into the room and asked if I could hold my breath for thirty seconds. He told me that they needed to look at my liver, too. I wasn't prepared to hear that. They had never scanned my liver before during a CT scan. Plus, my dad had just passed away six months earlier from liver cancer. I couldn't believe what I was hearing. They scanned my liver, and I couldn't wait to be on my way.

The week of my scan, the Lord had given me Psalm 27:1, "The Lord is my light and my salvation—whom shall I fear? The Lord is the stronghold of my life—of whom shall I be afraid?" (NIV) I read it over and over again. It gave me great peace.

The Saturday after my scan, I was feeling terrible. I wondered to myself again, *What if the cancer is back? Cancer number four.* It just didn't make sense to me, though. Why God would have given me the prayer shed idea with confirmation, if I wasn't going to be able to complete it?

While I was thinking about this, I got a call from another dear sister-in-Christ, Deb (a different Deb). I had called her earlier in the week and had asked for her prayers regarding the prayer shed. She told me she had called her sister in Pennsylvania and had told her about the prayer shed. Deb proceeded to tell me the incredible—her sister's neighbor in Pennsylvania had put a shed in her backyard for prayer and Bible study, and it was a huge hit. Deb's phone call was just the encouragement I needed. At that moment, I knew that someday the shed would be a reality for Jill and me. Deb's call convinced me that the shed idea wasn't a crazy idea at all. It was definitely God's idea, and He would see me through.

Through prayer, God's strength, and Deb's call, I made it through that weekend after my CT scan. On Monday, Jill went with me to my doctor's appointment. On the way to my appointment, she shared with me that she had read Psalm 30 that morning, the same Psalm I had read the day before. Psalm 30:9 says, "How can my dust in the grave speak out and tell the world about your faithfulness?" After reading that verse the day before, it had become my prayer. Jill and I felt God's presence.

When we got to the doctor's office, we prayed in the lobby. We tried hard to focus on the Lord and not the "what ifs." Within no time, we were in a room waiting for my nurse. When she arrived, she immediately shared the news with us—good news, terrific news! My scans were normal.

When the nurse left us with the good news, Jill and I rose to our feet, held hands and jumped up and down. We couldn't contain our excitement. Our hearts overflowed with joy and thanks to our faithful Heavenly Father. We knew then that the shed was no longer on the *distant* horizon . . . we knew that we needed to get to work.

That was in June of 1999. It is now August of 1999, and when I look out the back door of our house these days, I see a little shed named "Soul Purposes." Every time I see it, my heart fills with praise to God . . . the One who called us, guided us, (even to the name of the shed) and completely enabled us to accomplish what *He* had in mind.

So far, God's revealed plan for the shed is prayer and Bible study. We are anxious to see all that God will accomplish through a little prayer shed, which was built for His purposes and His glory. Praise be to God and His Son, our Savior and Lord, Jesus Christ.

Epilogue (to the Prayer Shed Story)

And now may the God of peace, who brought again from the dead our Lord Jesus, equip you with all you need for doing His will. (Hebrews 13:20, 21)

For those of you who are wondering . . . no, Pete didn't automatically go along with the prayer shed idea by any means. In fact, he had a major problem with it—he just didn't understand it at all. During that time, though, God brought Acts 5:29 to my mind almost daily, "We must obey God rather than men." And every time He did, I was strengthened and encouraged, determined to do His will. God also used Noah's story to encourage me then, too. With each passing day, I related to Noah more and more.

One day after a heated discussion with Pete regarding the shed, I said out loud while doing laundry, "How did you do it, Noah?!"

Later that afternoon, I came across a book I hadn't read in ages, *Children's Letters to God*, and I opened it up and read a letter by a little boy named Eddie. In that letter, Eddie wrote about how the bad people had laughed at Noah but that Noah was smart and had stuck with God. Before signing off, Eddie told God that he, too, would stick with Him. I, too, was determined to stick with God, and I asked friends to join me in prayer for Pete's heart to be changed.

With time and prayer, God changed Pete's heart. He also changed mine. God helped me to understand what Pete was feeling and to "give him a break," as one of my sisters-in-Christ said. She also told me—"It's not every day that people build prayer sheds in their back yard, T."

For my birthday, which fell during that time, Pete gave me a "saw" charm to add to my childhood charm bracelet. It was a symbol for the shed. I knew then that God had indeed changed Pete's heart, and my heart rejoiced. Weeks later, Pete built the prayer shed with our dear brother-in-Christ, Greg.

When I became a believer in Jesus Christ, I signed up for God's agenda, His plan for my life, whatever that plan might be. Since becoming a believer, I have been called to step out in faith many times in accomplishing God's purposes for my life. Building the prayer shed was one of those times.

No, it wasn't an ark like God called Noah to build, nor a wall like God called Nehemiah to build, nor a temple like God called Solomon to build, but still, it required a leap of faith for me and for Pete. And remembering Noah's ark, Nehemiah's wall and Solomon's temple, I sure am glad I was born in this time and this place. Pete has his limits . . .

The Piano

And my God will meet all your needs according to His glorious riches in Christ Jesus.
(Philippians 4:19, NIV)

One day, shortly after deciding to buy Agnes' house, we were discussing various things about the house with her. Agnes informed us then that the basement freezer, along with the piano, would go with the sale of the house—they would be ours. There just wasn't a way to get them out of the basement anymore.

Originally, Agnes and her family had lived in the basement of the house for several years until the rest of the house was finished. At that time, the laundry room had housed the kitchen, and the other basement rooms served as bedrooms.

(The house had been built during World War II, and getting wood for building was a problem back then.) At the time Agnes and her family had lived in the basement, there had been a basement door that opened to the outside. That's how they had originally gotten the freezer and the piano downstairs in the first place. Eventually, though, that basement door had been removed and cement block put in its place. Getting the freezer or the piano out of the basement just wasn't an option any longer. So whether we wanted them or not, they were ours.

At the time, we were glad to have "inherited" Agnes' freezer and her piano. We had always lived in apartments prior to buying Agnes' house, and the thought of being able to stock up on frozen items sounded good. And the piano, well, that sounded even better. I had never taken piano lessons before, but Pete had when he was younger. I also envisioned Zach, who was five years old at the time, taking lessons one day. I had no idea then, though, that the piano was really God's gift for *me*.

We had only lived in our new house for a short time when I was diagnosed with my second cancer. I prayed and prayed for God's grace to see me through my radiation and chemotherapy treatments. And His grace did see me through. Not only did I experience God's grace in a nurse named Grace, but I also experienced it through music—specifically through words and music God inspired me to write during that time.

As a teenager, I had written some simple songs while taking guitar lessons, but it had always been a struggle for me—matching the words and music, that is. During my second cancer and with God's inspiration, though, it was a totally different experience for me. The songs just flowed. Easily. Without a struggle. I felt that each inspired song was a special gift from God, a special kind of grace to see me through my cancer. When the songs came to me, I would run downstairs to, you guessed it, Agnes' old piano, where I would plunk out the simple tunes and then write them down before I forgot them.

Christmas came that year, and under the tree was a gift for me from Pete. I opened it up on Christmas Eve and found a gift certificate inside for piano lessons. Lessons that I took for six months that year from a delightful piano teacher named Joanne.

Although Agnes' piano had originally seemed like nothing more than an impossibility (as far as moving it was concerned), it was really an impossibility arranged by God to accomplish His purposes in my life. An impossibility that was, as they say, a possibility waiting to happen. For God knew that we didn't have a piano (before moving into Agnes' house), and He knew I would need one for the songs He would inspire me to write during that time.

Well, Agnes' piano remains in our basement still, and it still reminds me of two things. First, the fact that impossibilities are not always as they seem—that sometimes they really are possibilities waiting to happen. And second, I'm reminded that God will supply whatever I need for accomplishing His will. Even if it means sealing up a basement door so that a piano must be left behind . . .

Waiting on Him

Be still before the Lord and wait patiently for Him. (Psalm 37:7, NIV)

When I was involved with a care-giving ministry at our old church, an idea came to me. It seemed like a perfect fit. Ever since I was a child, I have loved to draw, and the idea was to design handmade cards to send to those being ministered to by the care-giving ministry. Cheery cards with Scripture verses, simple designs, and bright colors. I envisioned each caregiver from the ministry having an assortment of the cards at home. That way, when the caregiver wanted to send a card, he/she would have one on hand.

It was at one of our care-giving ministry brainstorming sessions that I eventually brought up the card idea. When the group heard the idea, there was some interest, but not enough to send me home to my drawing board! I couldn't believe it. To me, it had seemed like such a perfect fit. Handmade scripture cards for suffering people. When I had cancer the first time, cards encouraged me so much. Every time I needed a ray of hope in my day, there had been a card in the mailbox for me. Cards had been a lifeline to the outside world for me at that time.

I left the brainstorming session at church with my idea in hand. I felt disappointed, and I poured my heart out to God. I told Him that I wanted to use my talents for His glory and that I was willing to do the cards if that's what He wanted me to do.

Time went by, and then more time went by. Still I sensed nothing—no guidance, no confirmation . . . nothing. I began to believe that it just wasn't God's will for me at that time. But then, out of the blue one night at one of our meetings, I was asked if I could bring some samples of my cards. That's all I needed to hear to get my excitement going all over again! Yes! I told them I would bring some samples. No problem.

At the next meeting, with my cards on the table, there was an excitement in the air that I hadn't sensed at the earlier brainstorming session. As my cards were passed around, people shared their feelings regarding them, and we talked about how we would actually incorporate them into our ministry.

I left that meeting with renewed hope and excitement. Conversations regarding the cards continued at future meetings. One of our major decisions involved the production of the cards. Would we have them printed or would we color them ourselves? As we discussed the various options, a man's name came up, a man who at the time was a member of our church. Harry was his name, and he was an artist. It was suggested that I talk to Harry to get his opinions and possible help.

Well, Harry and I did talk, and it turned out that he knew a woman who owned a greeting card company. He suggested that we get together with her. Things were finally falling into place, and I was excited. Until, that is, our meeting with the woman Harry knew. The woman was very gracious, but we left that meeting without any new options. I was again disappointed.

On the way home, though, Harry thought of another printing company that he had worked with before, and we stopped by there, too. We talked to someone Harry knew, and he told us that he could print the cards. He also gave us the printing estimate. When I saw the quote, I knew that there was no way our church care-giving group had that kind of money in the budget. Again I was disappointed. Harry had been so helpful, but the idea just didn't seem to be working out. Again, I prayed. I was frustrated. I was freely offering my time and talents for use by God, but things just weren't working out. And God was silent. What was God's plan, anyway? I surely didn't have a clue. I decided that it just wasn't meant to be for some unknown reason. I would have to give up the idea.

During that same time, Pete and I had been praying for God to guide us to the church He wanted us to attend. We had occasionally been going to a church that our friends were attending then. In fact, they had been urging us to change churches. Was God directing us there? I wasn't convinced. But after several months of prayer, one night I felt an over-whelming sense of peace in regards to changing churches. The peace was so overwhelming that I was convinced it was indeed God's will for us at that time to change churches. After sharing my experience with Pete, he agreed. And although it wasn't easy saying goodbye to people we had grown to love at our old church, we knew God was directing and that we had to follow.

After some time had passed and we were at our new church, the card idea came to my mind again. I began praying about it anew. What was God's will? Eventually, God made it clear. I was to design, make and sell cards (with the help of a dear friend)—"Mission cards." The proceeds from the cards would go to missions, worldwide missions that helped to spread the good news about Jesus Christ.

I arranged a meeting with one of our new pastors to discuss the card idea. At the meeting, my friend and I showed examples of the cards and explained the missions tie-in. The pastor immediately liked the idea and arranged a follow-up meeting with someone else from church.

Soon after the second meeting, a "mission" card order was placed. Finally, it was God's will for me. His perfect timing had arrived.

Looking back, I clearly saw why the cards for the care-giving ministry never came to pass at our old church. God had known all along that just months later we would be attending another church.

The lesson of the cards was clear—I needed to wait on God and His perfect timing. It's a lesson I must return to often. Waiting is such a foreign concept to a world driven by almost instant everything. But as a believer, I am still called to wait on God (Psalm 27:14, 37:7, NIV) for the unfolding of His will, which, according to Romans 12:2, is "good, accept-able and perfect" (NRSV).

Waiting on God means choosing His will over my will. He created me, loves me more than I can imagine, knows me better than I know myself and knows the future I have yet to discover. Waiting on God means waiting for His best for me.

There was a TV show I watched as a child called "Father Knows Best." For us Christians, our Heavenly Father knows best. And I have found that waiting on Him is worth the wait . . . every single time.

The Prayer Group

The earnest prayer of a righteous man has great
power and wonderful results. (James 5:16b)

During September of 1997, I began a weekly Bible study with Jeanne, my dear sister-in-Christ. Our Bible study plan was to read through the entire Bible, to journal our thoughts as we read, and then to meet weekly to discuss our thoughts and questions. Hebrews 4:12 says, "For the word of God is living and active. Sharper than any double-edged sword, it penetrates even to dividing soul and spirit, joints and marrow; it judges the thoughts and attitudes of the heart" (NIV). Jeanne and I were anxious to hear what God had to personally say to each of us as we began our study that September.

Through my Bible reading and journaling, I began to feel God calling me to pray for the bigger issues of today, such as abortion. With every passing week, God's call to me got stronger.

As I specifically began to pray for the issues God had begun putting on my heart, an idea came to me one day. The idea was to start a prayer group, a prayer group that would join me in storming the gates of Heaven, regarding the bigger issues of this time and this place. As soon as the idea came to me, I began praying about the prayer group idea daily.

While I prayed during that time, several friends' names came to mind, and I decided to write them a letter. I told them about the prayer group idea and asked if they would be willing to give it some serious consideration and prayer. I mailed that letter on a Wednesday in January of 1998.

My dear friend and sister-in-Christ, Jill, was the first to respond to the letter. She was extremely excited about the idea of a prayer group and asked what other thoughts I had regarding it. I told her I was thinking of a group of six people who would pray individually during the month and then get together once a month to pray as a group. I told Jill that we needed to pray to see whether it was God's will for us at that time or not. She agreed to join me in prayer.

Like I mentioned earlier, my letter was mailed on a Wednesday. Well, the following Sunday came and we were at church. While glancing at the church bulletin before the service began, I read the sermon title for that Sunday, "What a Difference Praying Can Make." Was God going to speak to us already?! I eagerly anticipated the sermon . . .

Our pastor began his sermon by telling us some of the results of the early church's prayers—how the early church had been filled with awe and how the more believers prayed, the closer they became. True joy grew out of their prayers together, along with wonders and miracles. He also told us that the early church learned together, fellowshipped together and prayed together. He then gave us four prayer principles and closed by suggesting an idea. Why not start a prayer group with five or six individuals who would meet once a month for prayer? My heart leaped with joy and praise. I knew then that God was clearly speaking, and it was definitely His will for us to start a prayer group. When Jill heard the words of that sermon, she knew without a doubt, too, that God was clearly speaking.

In my earlier letter regarding my prayer group idea, I hadn't mentioned any specifics like the number of people to include or the number of meetings per month. But when Jill called after receiving the letter, she had asked what I specifically had in mind. At the time, only God knew how important those "specifics" would be in order for us to see His clear guidance during the sermon that Sunday.

The week following the prayer sermon, I excitedly called my other friends whom I had sent letters to. I told them about the sermon on prayer, and four of those friends committed to the prayer group.

The night before our first meeting to discuss any ideas for the group, I happened to read James 5:16b-18, "The earnest prayer of a righteous man has great power and wonderful results. Elijah was as completely human as we are, and yet when he prayed earnestly that no rain would fall, none fell for the next three and one half years! Then he prayed again, this time that it *would* rain, and down it poured and the grass turned green and the gardens began to grow again." That verse filled me with excitement and great anticipation.

At our meeting the next day, God's presence was evident. After the meeting, God continued to clearly guide us as well. He revealed to us the topics we were to pray about and how we were to pray (after we specifically asked Him)—with a clear conscience, boldly, earnestly, persistently, full of faith, and using Scripture. He also revealed specific prayers for each of the topics.

It has been both a blessing and a privilege to pray the prayers that God put on our hearts back then. Those prayers are big, but God is bigger. And although we haven't seen answers to all of those "big" prayers yet, we continue to pray.

For we believe Ephesians 3:20, which states, "Now glory be to God, who by His mighty power at work within us is able to do far more than we would ever dare to ask or even dream of—infinitely beyond our highest prayers, desires, thoughts, or hopes." We're trusting God for the answers. He's trusting us to pray . . .

God's Timing

For if you remain silent at this time, relief and deliverance for the Jews will arise from another place, but you and your father's family will perish. And who knows but that you have come to royal position for such a time as this? (Esther 4:14, NIV)

For weeks, a song I know kept coming to me that talks about coming into the kingdom of God for such a time, for such a time as this. It played over and over in my mind. I sensed God at work and asked Him to make clear what He was trying to get across to me. Nothing came to me, but the song persisted. I kept thinking to myself that I should read the book of Esther, since the song was based on that book of the Bible. But I didn't. It was a busy time with back-to-school activities, and during my devotional times, I read other things. And I forgot about the book of Esther.

During this time, one of our relatives had a heart attack. While I was concerned about her physical condition, I grew more and more concerned about her spiritual condition. Had she ever asked Jesus into her heart to be her Savior? I wasn't sure.

I talked to my dear sister-in-Christ, Deb, about the situation one day and she said, "T, you have to talk to her!" Well, maybe tomorrow, I thought to myself. When the next day came, it didn't seem that God was calling me to talk to her that day, either. It wasn't His timing, I decided. But Deb's words kept coming to me. Was there some sin that was preventing me from clearly hearing God's instructions to me?

A couple days after talking to Deb, I was in our basement. I was looking for books to put in the newly constructed prayer shed in our backyard when I came across a book I had ordered a long time before. It was one I had never gotten around to reading. It was a book of stories about women of the Bible. Paging through it, I was reminded that I hadn't read Esther's story yet. So I quickly checked to see if her story was included in the book and it was. I decided to sit down right then and read it.

As I read that story, God spoke to me so clearly through it. The following is what I read that day, "When Xerxes asked what she wanted, instead of blurting out the bad news about the edict and her people, she merely invited him and Hamann to a banquet. Xerxes quickly summoned Hamann and the three went off to the feast that Esther had prepared. Again, Xerxes asked Esther what she wanted. Again she invited him and Hamann to a second dinner the next day. Was she procrastinating? Or was she preparing the scene with great care? She and God's people had fasted and prayed for her encounter with the king. In some way God led her to know the right moment. That first banquet was not it."

God clearly confirmed to me through Esther's story that no, the timing hadn't been right yet to talk to our relative. My heart filled with praise, and I knew I had to continue to pray and wait on God and His perfect timing.

At church the following Sunday, I put in a prayer request for an opportunity to talk to our relative about spiritual matters. Our relative was scheduled to have surgery on a Monday, and the Friday before, I planned to see her at the hospital. I woke up that Friday morning and that song played in my mind again. The song about coming into the kingdom of God, for such a time as this. It played over and over in my mind, crowding out other thoughts. I could hardly think of anything other than that song. All of a sudden, I knew that God's perfect timing had arrived. He was calling me to talk to our relative that day.

Although I knew God would be with me, supplying me with just the right words, I was still apprehensive. Any previous spiritual talk with this relative always seemed to upset her. How in the world would I bring it up in the first place?! I prayed hard and I even called friends to pray before I left for the hospital that day. When I got there, it was just our relative, her roommate and me in the hospital room. We talked about a lot of things, and I silently prayed at the same time. I was praying so much, in fact, that I was surprised that some of those prayers didn't spill out into our conversation by mistake!

Soon, the roommate's family came to pick her up to go home. Our relative and I talked to them for quite awhile before they finally left.

After the roommate left, a sweet cleaning lady arrived, and I went to the bathroom. Inside the bathroom, I prayed and prayed for God's strength to bring up the spiritual subject. Yikes! I returned to our relative's side and the sweet cleaning lady was still there, cleaning without a word. I considered then that maybe she was an angel sent by God to strengthen me for the job at hand, to remind me that I wasn't alone—He was there.

God's perfect timing had arrived, and I knew I had to start talking. But suddenly, our relative said, "I think I'll take a nap now." *Oh, no!* I thought to myself. I knew I couldn't leave without sharing my thoughts with her. And so I began.

I told her then that I had been praying for her the night before and that morning. She asked me then what I had heard. I told her I couldn't leave without asking her a question, a question I had written to my dad in a letter before he died. And the question was, "Have you ever asked Jesus into your heart?" Her reply was quick. "No. You do it for me," she said. I told her I couldn't do it for her, and I asked her if she just wasn't ready or if she didn't think she needed to. She said she didn't think she needed to and that she had had the chance once before (to ask Jesus into her heart), but hadn't. I then mentioned John 1:12, "But to all who received Him, He gave the right to become children of God."

As the reality of her decision sunk in, I had tears in my eyes, and I told her that I wanted her to be in Heaven with me. She told me that she didn't believe in Heaven or Hell. And she said she didn't want me to get all upset about it and that maybe someday she would accept Jesus—but not now. She told me she was going to be fine. I told her that I, too, thought she would survive the operation. I also told her that I wasn't responsible for her decision regarding Jesus. I was just responsible for telling her.

She was amazingly calm during our conversation, and when I left her that day she told me to keep praying for her. I told her that I would. I felt so sad as I left her side that day at the hospital. Our conversation played over and over in my mind. Her salvation was truly a burden on my heart. I told myself over and over, though, that I wasn't responsible for her decision, and I told God that I would leave it with Him.

Over the next several days, I began to pray that she would be convinced of her sins so that she would see her need for a Savior. It seemed like I was praying for that even more of the time than I was for her physical healing. One day during that time, I questioned God whether I was praying the right prayers for her.

That night, I happened to pick up the same book in which I had earlier read Esther's story. I was drawn to the story about the woman at the well. Again, God confirmed things for me—part of the chapter about the woman at the well said, "Who could have guessed her inner thirst? Jesus knew and met her at the well of her life."

After reading this, I knew that yes, our relative had to be convinced of her sins, just like the woman at the well. And I asked Jesus then to meet our relative at the well of her life. Days following, I was even inspired to write a short song, and I began singing it daily, many times a day. "Meet her at the well of her life, oh Lord, convince her of her need for a Savior."

It's been a years now since I brought up the subject of a personal relationship with Jesus with my relative. Since that day, we have never talked about it again, but I continue to pray for her, trusting that God will meet her at the well of her life and convince her of her need for a Savior.

I was obedient to God that day in our relative's hospital room, and I leave the results with Him. Through Esther's obedience, God saved the Jewish nation from destruction. Who knows what He'll accomplish through my obedience or through your obedience. For we, too, like Esther, have been born "for such a time as this" (Esther 4:14, NIV).

Guided and Equipped

The Lord will work out His plans for my life—for your loving-kindness, Lord, continues forever. (Psalm 138:8)

Then everyone shall stand in awe and confess the greatness of the miracles of God; at last they will realize what amazing things He does. And the godly shall rejoice in the Lord, and trust and praise Him. (Psalm 64:9–10)

I'll never forget our pastor's sermon that first Sunday in November of 1998. During that sermon, I felt God's Holy Spirit at work. Afterwards, these words stayed with me: "Visions are powerful tools for what might happen in the future," and best of all were "visions with words and actions."

The day after hearing that sermon, I listened to my favorite radio pastor. His radio sermon series at the time was about Moses, one of my favorite biblical characters. And the radio pastor's words, as usual, drew me in.

Later that night, I was reading a fiction book from a popular series. In it, a certain devotional was mentioned. It was a devotional that I had actually purchased several years before. For some reason, after awhile, I put the book I was reading down and went to look for the devotional mentioned. I eventually discovered it in the wicker chest in our bedroom. Picking it up, I noticed a bookmark tucked between its pages. So I opened to that particular page and read. It, too, was about Moses.

The following days, I continued listening to the radio sermons about Moses. The more I heard the pastor speak of Moses, the more Moses' story seemed to be personally speaking to me. These words from the series stayed with me, just like my pastor's words on visions. "God will empower us to complete whatever He has called us to do. Some of you have been called by God to step out with a plan that seems treacherous."

I sensed that God was definitely at work, but I wasn't exactly sure what He was saying. I began to diligently pray that He would show me.

During that time, God reminded me of a prayer that I had been praying with my prayer group for months. Every Thursday since the beginning of that year, we had prayed for the cure for cancer. God had originally put the words "Pray for a cure" on my heart the first time I had cancer. I prayed for the cure occasionally back then, but most of my prayers focused on my own healing and not for the cure for cancer. With those thoughts on my mind, it dawned on me that the cure for cancer had been more and more of a burden on my heart since our prayer group had begun praying for it. I realized then that I had been praying for the cure with greater and greater intensity. And not just on Thursdays. I also realized that my pastor's words regarding visions and the radio pastor's words about Moses were still on my mind. What was God's will? I wondered . . .

I decided to write our pastor to let him know my thoughts regarding praying for the cure, visions and Moses' story. He wrote back and suggested that I meet with Vicki, our prayer pastor, to determine God's will. I called Vicki to set up an appointment.

Vicki and I met, and I shared my thoughts with her. During our meeting, Vicki mentioned that the following spring she had a prayer concert scheduled on the church calendar. At that time, though, she didn't know what the prayer concert would focus on. She suggested that we could pray for the cure for cancer then. We also committed it to God and asked Him to guide us according to His will.

After my meeting with Vicki, I continued searching the Scriptures for insight, and the following verses seemed to jump off the pages at me when I read them. "For nothing is impossible with God" (Luke 1:37, NIV). "Now go ahead and do as I tell you, for I will help you to speak well, and I will tell you what to say" (Exodus 4:12). "With God's help we shall do mighty things, for He will trample down our foes" (Psalm

60:12). "How we thank you, Lord! Your mighty miracles give proof that you care" (Psalm 75:1). "Now glory be to God who by His mighty power at work within us is able to do far more than we would ever dare to ask or even dream of—infinitely beyond our highest prayers, desires, thoughts, or hopes" (Ephesians 3:20). "But the Lord said, 'Go and do what I say" (Acts 9:15a). "Yes, I will bless the Lord and not forget the glorious things he does for me. He forgives all my sins, He heals me" (Psalm 103:2–3).

I sensed over time that God was saying, "Yes! Plan the prayer concert." And my excitement grew.

In the midst of my excitement over God's apparent plan, Satan began attacking me and filling me with questions and doubts. Dad had cancer at the time and, according to his doctor, wouldn't live much longer. What if Dad was really sick when the prayer concert was scheduled in March? Or what if he even passed away during that time? Those questions whirled and whirled around in my mind, trying to drown me in a swamp of confusion.

Psalm 139 says that the Lord knows my thoughts from far away. One morning, aware of my thoughts regarding Dad, God graciously directed me to Luke 9:59–60 and clearly spoke to me through it: "Another time, when He invited a man to come with Him and to be His disciple, the man agreed—but wanted to wait until His father's death. Jesus replied, 'Let those without eternal life concern themselves with things like that. Your duty is to come and preach the coming of the Kingdom of God to all the world.'" I knew at that moment that I had to follow the Lord's leading and that

He would take care of the details. His call was to *me,* and I had to obey. (God knew then what I didn't. He knew that Dad would pass away November 28, a short time later, months before the prayer concert.)

When I met with Vicki again, she said she hadn't received any concrete confirmation from God regarding "Pray for the Cure." But we would proceed with prayer, praying that God would close doors if it wasn't His will for us to do it. At the meeting, Vicki also asked me to write out some specific prayers for the prayer concert.

One night after my meeting with Vicki, I prayed for God to specifically show me through Scripture whether the "Pray for the Cure" prayer concert was truly His will or not. The next day, I prayed again, before searching for verses I could use for the prayers Vicki had asked me to write for the prayer concert. While searching the Scriptures that morning, I remembered a verse in Jeremiah that I could use, Jeremiah 32:27, "I am the Lord, the God of all mankind; is there anything too hard for me?" After writing it down, my eyes skipped over to the other column of verses on that same page. And I read, "Then I knew for sure that the message I had heard was really from the Lord" (Jeremiah 32:8b). God had heard my prayer from the previous night and confirmed His will through Jeremiah 32:8b! My heart danced with praise. I was excited to be a part of His plan.

Every day quickly somersaulted into the next as Vicki and I planned the prayer concert under God's direction. The specific schedule for the evening was arranged, music selected and prayers written. Posters were designed, made and then distributed around the city. Programs for the special evening were also designed and made. God even inspired me with a song for the prayer concert, too. During that time, Vicki and I were also invited to be on a local Christian radio show, to be interviewed regarding "Pray for the Cure."

The day before the interview, I was sick and I wondered how I would ever be able to do the interview feeling like I did. During my quiet time that morning, I prayed for God's healing touch. After praying, God directed me to Hebrews 13: 20–21, "And now may the God of peace, who brought again from the dead our Lord Jesus, equip you with all you need for doing His will." I knew then that God would somehow see me through. He would equip me with all I needed for doing His will, at least for the hour that we were on the air! And He did.

After the radio interview, the prayer concert was within a week, and I found myself in the middle of spiritual warfare. I recovered from the bug I had, but then days before the prayer concert, I began getting optic migraine headaches—a migraine headache that is accompanied by wavy lines that dance across the eyes, leaving one virtually "blind" until the wavy lines disappear, at which time the painful headaches begin. I'd had a few optic migraines in my life but not for years.

My optic migraine reminded me of the words of a doctor at the University of Minnesota to whom I had gone years ago. "Lie down for twenty minutes as soon as the lines appear and you won't get the headache." So every time the wavy lines appeared, I quickly lay down. My dear sister-in-Christ, Deb, called during that time, and after I told her about the optic migraines, she asked how much estrogen I was on. When I told her, she couldn't believe the seemingly high amount I took every day, and she suggested my migraines could be a result of the estrogen.

Just one day before the prayer concert I had another migraine, and I panicked. I quickly called my doctor to explain the situation. My doctor wasn't on call that Saturday, but the doctor I talked to agreed to prescribe some migraine medication. I also mentioned the estrogen level I was on and he agreed the estrogen could be causing the migraines.

Sunday arrived and Pete, Zach and I went to church in the morning. After lunch, wavy lines started to appear and I quickly lay down. Every time I tried getting up, the lines returned. The prayer concert was only hours away. I fervently prayed again for God's help and healing touch.

The Holy Spirit then reminded me of Hebrews 13:20–21, the verse I had read before the radio interview. I trusted that somehow God would equip me with all I needed for doing His will, just like He always had in the past.

Before leaving home for the prayer concert, I took some migraine medication since I knew I wouldn't be able to lie down during the concert. When we got to church, I told Vicki about my optic migraine and together we called out to God for help. After praying I still felt like I was on the verge of a migraine. Until, that is, the prayer concert started. Once it started, I felt fine. Once again, I was equipped by God to do His will.

That night during the prayer concert we felt God's powerful and awesome presence among us. We were before God's throne, humbled by His presence, full of praise and thanksgiving, praying for the cure for cancer. God heard our prayers, and we were blessed. God's will was done that night, His purposes accomplished.

I, along with others, continue to pray for the cure for cancer, trusting that God will send the cure—in His perfect way, in His perfect timing. We are anxiously awaiting a miracle.

There are some today who don't believe in miracles. I personally met one of them at the Pray for the Cure prayer concert. But according to Mark 6:5 that's nothing new: "And because of their unbelief [Jesus] couldn't do any mighty miracles among them except to place His hands on a few sick people and heal them."

Psalm 77:13–14 says, "O God, your ways are holy. Where is there any other as mighty as you? You are the God of miracles and wonders! You still demonstrate your awesome power." Yes, God still demonstrates His awesome power. He is the God of miracles and wonders who waits for us to believe . . .

P.S. The following are the prayers from the night of the prayer concert . . .

> *I pray that you will begin to understand how incredibly great his power is to help those who believe in him. (Ephesians 1:19)*

Our understanding of you is limited, O God. Our finite minds cannot fully comprehend you, our infinite God. We are weak. You are strong. We are limited. You are limitless. We have some knowledge. You are all-knowing. Pour out your grace upon us and give to all an understanding of how incredibly great your power is to help those who believe. WE PRAY, LORD, FOR A CURE FOR CANCER.

> *For nothing is impossible with God. (Luke 1:37, NIV)*

The Bible tells us, O God, that you spared Noah from the raging floodwaters that you sent upon the earth and that you sealed the mouths of the lions surrounding Daniel in the lions' den. We have read how you saved Jonah's life in the belly of the fish and how by your power, young David conquered Goliath with a slingshot and a stone. For the Israelites, you parted the Red Sea and rained bread from heaven for them to eat while they were in the wilderness. In your Word, examples abound of impossible situations. Cancer is an impossible situation today, Lord. We believe by faith, that nothing is impossible with you and WE PRAY, LORD, FOR A CURE FOR CANCER.

> *Now glory be to God who by his mighty power at work within us is able to do far more than we would ever dare to ask or even dream of—infinitely beyond our highest prayers, desires, thoughts, or hopes. (Ephesians 3:20)*

We admit, O Lord, that many times our prayers aren't big enough. We pray for that which is possible and don't consider praying for that which is impossible. But impossibilities are your specialty, O God, and your resources are unlimited. Your Word says that you are able to do far more than we would ever dare to ask or even dream of. We know that a cure for cancer is a big request, but we know the One in whom we trust, and we believe that nothing is impossible with you. WE PRAY, O LORD, FOR A CURE FOR CANCER.

> *I am the Lord, the God of all mankind, is there anything too hard for me? (Jeremiah 32:27)*

O Lord, you are the God of all mankind, Creator of heaven and earth. All things in heaven and on earth came into being by your command; by your breath we were given life. We stand in awe of you and all that you have created. Your works are wonderful. Your glory fills the earth. O, Lord, there is none like you, and we believe that nothing is too hard for you. WE PRAY, O LORD, FOR A CURE FOR CANCER.

> *So let us come boldly to the very throne of God and stay there to receive his mercy and to find grace to help us in our times of need. (Hebrews 4:16)*

Through Jesus Christ's death on the cross, we have peace with you, O Lord God, and because we have been washed in the blood of Jesus, we come boldly before your throne. We are humbled by your presence, yet we come boldly, aware of who we are in Christ Jesus. Cancer has ravaged the bodies of many we love. You see our pain. You know our needs and our hearts' desires. Out of your boundless mercy and grace WE PRAY, O LORD, FOR A CURE FOR CANCER.

> *O Lord God! You have made the heavens and*
> *earth by your great power; nothing is too hard*
> *for you. (Jeremiah 32:17)*

Delicate snowflakes, gentle rain, breathtaking mountains, glorious sunsets, twinkling stars, fragile butterflies, fragrant flowers, mighty oceans. We stand, O Lord God, in awe of your creation. You formed it all by your great power. Who can compare to you? Nothing is too hard for you. Not even the cure for cancer. WE PRAY, O LORD, FOR A CURE FOR CANCER.

> *Praise the Lord, O my soul, and forget not all his*
> *benefits—who forgives all your sins and heals*
> *all your diseases, who redeems your life from the*
> *pit and crowns you with love and compassion,*
> *who satisfies your desires with good things so*
> *that your youth is renewed like the eagles.*
> *(Psalm 103:2–5)*

You, O Lord, are great. You alone deserve unending worship and praise. May we never forget all your benefits, Lord, and your daily care for each of us. The Bible tells us that you heal all our diseases, out of your boundless mercy. Father, we pray now for the medical community, for the research teams that are working on finding the cure for cancer. May you speak to them and through them. We thank you for good and capable doctors, nurses, and care-givers. Give them wisdom and encouragement in light of the difficulties that they face every day. Father, thank you for the treatment that is available, and thank you for the providers. May we step out in faith and call you the Great Physician, all-powerful, compassionate, all-sufficient. May our faith in you be strengthened. May your will be done on earth, as it is in heaven. LORD, WE PRAY FOR A CURE FOR CANCER.

The Day After 9/11

Cast your burden on the Lord, and He will sustain you; He will never permit the righteous to be moved. (Psalm 55:22, NRSV)

It's now October 11, 2001, one month after the heinous terrorist attacks on the World Trade Center and the Pentagon. Images of that day are still being replayed in my mind. But another image is being replayed, too. An image sent from Heaven above on September 12, 2001, one day after the tragedy . . .

Pete, Zach and I were in the church parking lot the evening of September 12, walking to our car. I had just attended a prayer service while Pete and Zach were involved elsewhere on the church campus. Although the prayer service I attended was inspirational and encouraging, I still felt a deep sense of sadness surrounding me as we made our way to the car. The horrible events of the day before remained heavy on my heart.

Almost to our car, we saw a man and a little boy approaching us. When we got closer to them, we noticed that the little boy, who was about a year and a half old, was walking with his diaper bag hung around his neck. The diaper bag was almost touching the ground and the little boy kept stumbling over it. The man, who I assume was his daddy, tried to help by taking the diaper bag from him. When he did, the little boy protested by crying and repeatedly pushing his daddy away, determined to carry that heavy bag himself.

As we walked past them, Pete smiled and said to the daddy, "That's a pretty heavy load for a little guy." The daddy answered, "He *wants* to carry it." Those words stayed with me as we continued walking.

At the car, I opened the door and got in. While buckling my seatbelt, something occurred to me. I realized then that the image we had just witnessed was an incredible example of how we at times hang onto and carry our burdens, instead of handing them over to God, our Heavenly Father. I sensed then that it was an image sent from above.

At that moment, God spoke to me personally. He revealed to me then that I had been hanging onto my burdens, my sadness, my grief over the events of September 11. I, like that little boy, needed to give my burdens to my Father. For just like that little boy's daddy, my Heavenly Father was reaching down, longing to help.

The images of September 11, 2001, are forever etched in my mind. But so is the image of that little boy and his daddy in our church parking lot. An image I have returned to many times since September 12, 2001. An image that continues to remind me that I'm not alone—that my Heavenly Father is right beside me on my journey this side of heaven. An image that also reminds me that my heavenly Father longs to help, to carry my burdens so that I won't stumble and fall under the weight. Finally, it's an image of the action I need to take to experience God's peace, even in the midst of life's worst storms. And that action is to give my "diaper bag"—my burdens to the Lord. To give my "diaper bag"—my burdens to the Lord. "Cast your burden on the Lord, and He will sustain you; He will never permit the righteous to be moved" (Psalm 55:22, NRSV).

Ending

I came that they may have life and have it abundantly. (John 10:10, NRSV)

Abundant (Adj.)—1a: marked by great plenty b. amply supplied: abounding

2: occurring in abundance.

Early one morning after taking a shower, the song "My Redeemer Lives" came to me. It seemed to come to me from out of the blue, and when it did, I began singing it.

While upstairs drying my hair, the song continued playing in my mind. At one point, I felt as if I would burst if I didn't sing it out loud . . . loudly! I thought I might scare Zach's friend Michael, though, who was waiting for him just down the hall. So instead, I quietly sang it out loud. *Why was it coming to me?* I wondered.

In the afternoon, I sat down to do some writing. I was actually going to write the ending for this book. Before starting, I prayed for God's help. After writing for some time, though, I realized that it just wasn't coming together like usual. So, I put my pen and paper away for the day. I also prayed again for God's help.

Later that afternoon, I dropped Zach off at a friend's house. Driving home, the song from that morning returned to me. When it did, I started singing it again. As I sang, I realized why it had been playing on my mind. It was the perfect ending for this book!

I was amazed when I considered that God had delivered the ending for the book hours before I needed it—I just hadn't realized it at the time. As I drove, I continued singing . . .

My Redeemer lives
My Redeemer lives
My Redeemer lives
My Redeemer lives

You lift my burden
I'll rise with You
I'm dancin' on this mountaintop
to see Your kingdom come.

Jesus said, "I came that they may have life, and have it abundantly" (John 10:10, NRSV).

Since January of 1992 when I began a personal relationship with Jesus, I have lived an abundant life; a full life. Even in the crucible of cancer. In Him I have found physical and spiritual healing, forgiveness for my sins, deliverance from the guilt and power of sin, eternal life, relief from my burdens, unconditional love, satisfaction, refreshment when I'm weary, peace and joy regardless of my circumstances, power to do God's will, strength when I am weak, meaning and purpose for my life and guidance for my days. I stand in awe of all that God is and all that He has done for me through His Son Jesus Christ.

Yes, my Redeemer lives, and because of Him, I am living an abundant life. I am expectantly waiting and "dancin' on this mountaintop" to see His kingdom come . . . for I believe the best is yet to come. How about you?

God never forces Himself into our life's picture. Rather, He waits for us to admit our need and to ask Jesus to be our Savior and Lord of our lives. When we choose to receive Jesus, we welcome God Himself into our life's picture, and God smiles. And when God smiles in the picture of our lives, it's a beautiful picture. No doubt about it.

With God in the Picture of My Life ...

💜 my life's picture is vibrant and colorful ... no longer dull and lifeless.

💜 my life's picture is focused ... no longer fuzzy like when I was unsure of my real purpose in life.

💜 my life's picture is full of meaning ... no longer empty and meaningless.

💜 my life's picture is the perfect size ... no longer reaching for more or settling for less than God has for me.

💜 my life's picture is filled with the faces of others ... no longer a self-portrait.

💜 my life's picture is the perfect picture ... regardless of the background set of circumstances.

💜 my life's picture is eternal and will never fade ... no longer headed for eternal destruction.

💜 my life's picture is taken at the right speed ... taking time to enjoy the gift of each new day.

💜 my life's picture is shot with the right lens (perspective is everything!) ... no longer just seeing things from my limited earthly perspective but rather seeing things from God's heavenly perspective.

💜 my life's picture has a supernatural shine to it ... which is actually joy—joy that overflows because of my relation-ship with Jesus.

💜 my life's picture is peaceful ... no longer filled with fear.

But I trust in your unfailing love;
my heart rejoices in your salvation.
I will sing to the Lord, for He has been good to me.
Psalm 13:5–6 (NIV)

End Notes

1. *Holy, Holy, Holy* lyrics by Reginald Heber (1783-1826), (p. 32)

2. "Taken from *Streams in the Desert* by L.B. Cowman. Copyright © 1997 by The Zondervan Corporation. Used by permission of Zondervan." (p. 53)

3. I LIFT MY EYES UP (PSALM 121) © 1990 Vineyard Songs Canada (Administered By Mercy/Vineyard Publishing in the U.S.) (ASCAP) "All Rights Reserved. Used By Permission." (p.112)

4. *I Am Here With You* by David J. Schut, copyright 1999. Used by permission of David J. Schut. (pp.121, 122)

5. *Unto the Hills* by Billy Graham, copyright 1996. Used by permission of Thomas Nelson, Inc. (p.124)

6. "Taken from *Streams in the Desert* by L.B. Cowman. Copyright © 1997 by The Zondervan Corporation. Used by permission of Zondervan." (p.136)

7. Taken from *Streams in the Desert* by L.B. Cowman. Copyright © 1997 by The Zondervan Corporation. Used by permission of Zondervan." (p.137)

8. GREAT EXPECTATIONS © PEACH HILL SONGS 2/ SPARROW SONG. "All Rights Reserved. Used By Permission." (p.160)

9. "conform." *Merriam-Webster Online Dictionary*. 2002. http://www.Merriam-Webster.com (6 Sept. 2003). (p. 201)

10. Dennis J. DeHaan. *Our Daily Bread*, copyright 1994. Used by permission of RBC Ministries. (p. 210)

11. "Taken from *Streams in the Desert* by L.B. Cowman. Copyright © 1997 by The Zondervan Corporation. Used by permission of Zondervan." (pp. 218, 222)

12. *A Woman God Can Use/A Woman Jesus Can Teach* by Alice Mathews, © 1990. Used by permission of Discovery House Publishers. (pp. 248, 251)

13. "abundant." *Merriam-Webster Online Dictionary*. 2002. http://www. Merriam-Webster.com (6 Sept. 2003) (p. 265)

14. *REDEEMER* by Nicole C. Mullen © 2000 Lil' Jas' Music (Admin. by Wordspring Music, LLC), Wordspring Music, LLC. All Rights Reserved. Used By Permission. (p. 266)

About the Author

T. Windahl is an inspirational speaker and writer who loves God, His Word and His people. Since personally encountering God in January 1992 and experiencing the transforming power of His unconditional love, her life has been marked by joy and thanksgiving. After T's encounter with God, and in answer to prayer, God revealed His purpose for her life: to be a light of His love and truth to those around her and to those she meets. She loves to laugh and delights in catching glimpses of God at work in her life and in the lives of others. She thoroughly enjoys being a wife and mom, encouraging others, reading, using her artistic talents and spending time with family and friends at a local coffee shop in Minnetonka, Minnesota.

To contact the author:
T. Windahl
P.O. Box 870
Hopkins, MN 55343